CONFLICTS

CONFLICTS

*Studies in
Contemporary History*

BY

LEWIS BERNSTEIN NAMIER

Essay Index Reprint Series

BOOKS FOR LIBRARIES PRESS
FREEPORT, NEW YORK

First Published 1942
Reprinted 1969

STANDARD BOOK NUMBER:
8369-1230-6

LIBRARY OF CONGRESS CATALOG CARD NUMBER:
73-90667

PRINTED IN THE UNITED STATES OF AMERICA

PREFACE

WITH the single exception of one article published twenty-four years ago, all the essays in this book were written since the outbreak of the present war, and even the least contentious among them bears the marks of recent severe Conflicts. All have been printed before, and are now republished with a minimum of change; their original dates should therefore be noted.

My best thanks are due to the editors, owners, and publishers for permission to reproduce the essays.

L. B. NAMIER

15 GLOUCESTER WALK
LONDON, W.8
Spring, 1942

CONTENTS

	PAGE
FROM VIENNA TO VERSAILLES	1
AFTER VIENNA AND VERSAILLES	19
THE GERMAN INTERNATIONAL	34
HITLER'S WAR	53
1812 AND 1941	62
SYMMETRY AND REPETITION	69
THE MISSING GENERATION	73
GERMANY	78
I. National Character	
II. Names and Realities	
III. Both Slaves and Masters	
"IN TIMES OF CONFUSION"	94
"SURVEY OF INTERNATIONAL AFFAIRS, 1938".	102
THE JEWS	121
NUMBERS AND EXODUS	137
JUDAICA	163
TWO BOOKS ON EASTERN EUROPE	174
I. The Ukraine	
II. Carpatho-Russia	
DEMOCRACY	186

CONTENTS

	PAGE
THE PARTY SYSTEM	197
I. The Crown and the Party System	
II. The Two-Party System	
III. Democracy and Party	
GOVERNMENT IN WAR-TIME	210
ENGLISH PROSE	217

FROM VIENNA TO VERSAILLES

(" *The Nineteenth Century and After* ", February 1940)

I

In time and space, the scene of nineteenth-century European history lay between Vienna and Versailles: the century opened in 1815 and closed in 1919, and Europe extended from the Channel ports to the western frontiers of Russia and Turkey. Great Britain and Russia were in Europe but not of Europe, and between 1815 and 1914 actively intervened in European conflicts only when Turkey was concerned, an Asiatic Power which in the Eastern Mediterranean held the key position between three continents.

European interests and entanglements have defeated the extra-European expansion of the Continental nations. The nations which stand at the two ends of the European chain — England, Spain and Portugal, and Russia — have given their languages to the " white man's lands " outside Europe and have built up empires and supplied most of their population, while those in the centre, or facing inland seas, exhausted their strength in contests over strips of land on the smallest and most densely populated of continents. Spain turned her face to Europe and, while contesting the Mediterranean, lost the oceans — by 1815 she had ceased to count even in European affairs; and so had

Sweden, having during the preceding two centuries contested, conquered, and lost the Baltic. Between 1815 and 1914, more than ever before, European politics were focussed between Vienna and Versailles.

France and Russia span Europe from north to south — the one at its narrow, tapering end, the other where the European peninsula passes into the great Eurasian continent: France, marvellously diversified and yet coherent, articulated in her geographical structure, Russia, a vast empire, remarkably uniform and featureless for its size. In the centre of Europe the Alps interpose between north and south, dividing Germany from Italy. Between Central Europe and the great Russian plain, from Karelia to Morea, stretches a region broken up by seas and mountains into a maze of geographical formations: the European Middle East, the belt of small nations.

In 1815 the West, North, and East of Europe were the spheres of nationally consolidated States: Great Britain, France, Spain, Portugal, the Scandinavian countries, and Russia — each practically of one language only,[1] comprising all, or almost all, who spoke that language and who could, or wished to, be included. The two great nations of Central Europe, the Germans and the Italians, burdened with a Pan-European past and with its heirs and exponents, the Habsburgs, remained in a condition of political disunion and dynastic subdivision; while the smaller nationalities of East-Central Europe, which by 1920 came to form (not counting Turkey) twelve independent States (two

---

[1] In 1815 Poland and Finland were joined to, but not incorporated in, Russia.

of them, moreover, of a composite character—Czechoslovakia and Yugoslavia), were as yet all engulfed in the Habsburg Monarchy, the Ottoman Empire, and in the western fringe of Russia. Union (or separation) in monolinguistic national States became in the nineteenth century the political aim of the educated, and in time of the semi-educated, classes in Europe — of European nationalisms.

All the engulfed nationalities had, at some time, formed States of their own; and they all preserved the memory, though only some retained the social foundations and the intellectual habits, of an independent political existence. Numerous shadowy outlines of defunct States and Empires covered the map of East-Central Europe, cutting existing frontiers and intercrossing each other: the heirs to these memories and traditions tried to put new life and contents into the ancient shapes. Two of these previous States were only half submerged — Poland and Hungary; and even while half submerged, the Poles and Magyars continued to assert claims to political dominion over territories inhabited by an alien population which had remained socially and economically subject to them.

II

Most frontier problems in Europe are due to incomplete conquests in the past; and most of the European conquests are part of a great overland expansion, an almost universal Continental " *Drang nach Osten* ". The original tide of migrations, at the close of the Roman era and in the early Middle Ages, proceeded from east and north to west and south, pressing into the long bag of the European peninsula and overflowing into Africa. The movement continued on the circumference in the migrations of the Norsemen over seas and along rivers, of the Arabs across North Africa, and in successive waves of Mongol invaders (Huns, Avars, Magyars, Tartars, and Turks) which long continued to break over Eastern and South-Eastern Europe, causing eddies and cross-currents after the direction of the main movement had been reversed. For the Romanised, or at least Christianised, West was the first to harden once more into organised nations which, one by one, proceeded to expand into the less populated and more backward territories to the east of their own; and this movement continued into the nineteenth, or even into the twentieth, century. The French pressed against the Germans and the Italians, the Germans against the Western Slavs (of whom only the Poles and Czechs survived as nations) and against the Lithuanians; the Poles and Lithuanians against the western branches of the Russian nation; the Russians against the Finnish and Mongol tribes of Eurasia; the Spaniards across the Western Mediterranean, the Italians across the Adriatic, the Swedes across the Baltic. The face of all these nations was to the east, at certain times to meet a danger, but more often to take advantage of the much greater opportunities for expansion and colonisation which offered in that direction; but expansion to the east entailed for these nations a weakening of their defence against pressure from the west.

Each conquest was integral within certain districts,

partial over much wider areas. In the case of partial conquests the upper classes and the urban population were as a rule the first to be replaced or assimilated by the conquerors, while the peasantries retained their original nationality. Every Ireland had its Ulster, its towns of " the Pale ", its Anglo-Irish gentry, and its peasantry, which, wherever it has survived, in the long run gets the better of the other classes — a returning, reconquering tide. There was a time when the Irish Protestants claimed to be the Irish nation; when to the Swedes Finland was Swedish; when the Germans talked about " *das deutsche Baltikum* " and looked upon the whole of Western Austria from Reichenberg to Trieste as German; when in considering the Partitions of Poland, neither the Poles nor even most other nations distinguished between the carving-up of ethnic Poland and the recovery by Russia of provinces with a mere Polish veneer. Every single one of these imperialist claims was justified so long as the nationality of the upper and middle classes determined that of the country, while the peasant masses, serf or semi-serf, counted politically for no more than their cattle. Even the French Revolution, while proclaiming the equality of all men, at the start divided them into " active " and " passive " citizens; under the Restoration some conservative thinkers tried to revive an ideological distinction between " *la nation* " and " *le peuple* "; and " *le pays légal* " of the July Monarchy still expressed the difference which, even in the most advanced countries, continued to exist in practice, long after it had disappeared from political theory.

An ethnic map of the territories intervening between

the Germans and the Great Russians, drawn in 1815 and based on the language of the upper and middle classes, would have been in four colours only. The Baltic provinces, the whole of East Prussia and Silesia, Bohemia and Moravia, and the Slovene provinces would have been counted as German; the Adriatic littoral as Italian; Lithuania, Latgalia, White Russia, and the Western Ukraine, including East Galicia, as Polish; and practically the whole of Hungary as Magyar. Here were four nations which over adjacent territories spread out fine-meshed nets embroidered with patches of solid material; every conquest had been accompanied by a certain measure of integral colonisation which followed lines of minor resistance or of greater economic advantage, and which left ragged frontiers and scattered settlements of conquerors among a subject population. The partial successes of the past have burdened these nations with doubtful, dangerous assets which they are loth to write off. It is hard for any nation to renounce territory which it has been accustomed to consider its own, and this is the harder the greater the proportion which such territory forms of its total area, and the more it still lives in the social and political ideas of the privileged " political nation ".[1] The Italians held but a narrow fringe beyond their solid ethnic settlements. The German octopus extended one arm far along the Baltic, another up the Oder, a third down the Danube, dominating, permeating, encircling non-German territories; still, considerable

[1] So long as the nobility and gentry were dominant in this country and owned most of the land in Ireland, it was difficult for Great Britain to renounce Southern Ireland, the inheritance and possession of these classes.

though the area was of partial German conquests (and beyond it lay an even wider area of haphazard, scattered German colonisation), it formed but a fraction of Germany's territorial holdings. In Hungary the part of the country containing Magyar enclaves or covered by a thin Magyar veneer exceeded in area and population that of the integral Magyar settlements; while east of ethnic Poland, the Polish aristocracy and landed gentry covered territory twice its size, with almost double its population.

III

What national States should arise in Central and East-Central Europe, and in what frontiers? — this was the main territorial problem of the nineteenth century. It was seemingly solved after the last war, and is reopened to-day.

There was a logic and a rhythm in the consecutive changes. The problem naturally first came up for discussion and solution in the terms in which it was envisaged by the " master nations ". They staked out their claims, demanding union of all their branches, and disregarding the interests and denying the rights of the subject races. The prescriptive rights of dynasties, especially of the Habsburgs, were at that time the chief obstacle to the national programmes of the Germans, Italians, and Magyars; the territorial claims of these three nations were non-competing, nor did they clash in Austria with those of the Poles. By 1870 the Germans, Italians, and Magyars had realised the essence of their national programmes, and so had the

Poles within the narrow framework of Galicia. The Habsburgs, who in 1848 had played off the subject races against the " master nations ", now settled down to a condominium with these nations, and, while still at times using the others as a check upon their new partners, they never again seriously challenged the German-Magyar-Polish basis of their reconstructed Empire. The Habsburg Monarchy and the dominion of the Germans and Magyars in Austria-Hungary collapsed together. In terms of the Habsburg possessions the history of the nineteenth century can be summed up in three dates, of which the middle one bisects the period that intervenes between Vienna and Versailles, and in three names — 1815, the Austrian Empire; 1867, Austria-Hungary; 1919, the Succession States.

Opposed to the Poles and their programme were Prussia and Russia. The conflict with Prussia turned on fundamental geographical contradictions: in Posnania Polish ethnic settlements cut deep between two of the arms which Germany stretches out to the east, and, following the Vistula, Polish settlements interpose between Pomerania and East Prussia. The conflict with Russia turned on Poland's dominion over vast stretches of land inhabited by White Russian and Little Russian peasantries. Destroyed politically in the Partitions of Poland, it survived in the complete social and economic superiority of the Polish upper classes over their peasant serfs. Poland's dominion over these provinces was perhaps the main cause of her original downfall, and Polish demands for its re-establishment, pressed with passionate insistence, were the greatest obstacle to her resurrection. Tsarist Russia, perhaps because it did not concede political rights even to the upper and middle classes, combined, in a peculiar though contradictory manner, support for dynasties and serf-owning nobles with a protectorate over Slav and Greek-Orthodox peasantries: it thus sponsored the rights of " subject nationalities " against their masters, opposed the reconstruction of Poland, and worked for the disruption of Austria-Hungary and Turkey. But by an irony of fate and a deeper logic, the problem of the entire European Middle East, from Karelia to Morea, covering the Habsburg and Ottoman Empires and the western fringe of Russia, came up for discussion and solution in ethnic terms within the same decade. Together with the submerged subject nationalities re-arose Poland, drawing for herself a frontier across White Russian and Ukrainian territory in accordance with the ideas held by the " master nations " about the middle of the nineteenth century rather than with the principles of 1920.

Reviewed in terms of repose and action, the ninety-nine years which intervene between the Congress of Vienna and the outbreak of the World War fall into three almost equal periods: 1815–1848, 1848–1878, and 1878–1914. The first was a time of peace and rest after the great convulsion of the Revolutionary and Napoleonic Wars: it was the era of Metternich and of the Holy Alliance, of a conservative settlement based on principles which favoured the Habsburgs but were supported by Prussia and Russia on grounds of a common anti-revolutionary, monarchical interest. The authority of the Habsburgs rested on dynastic property in States and territories; this was a negation of popular sovereignty, therefore of any right to self-government or to national self-determination. In Germany and in Italy the safeguarding of dynastic rights meant a continuance of national disunion, which in turn safeguarded Habsburg predominance; within the allodial possessions of the Habsburgs it meant a continuance of their rule over a polyglot Empire of which they were the bond of union.

Thirty-three years went by, the working life of a generation. In 1848, the *annus mirabilis* of European history, a movement arose which shook the core of Europe from Versailles to Vienna, and called in question the very existence of the Habsburg Monarchy. As in all true revolutions, there arose the illusion of infinite possibilities; a creative spirit seemed to brood over chaos, about to give birth to new worlds. Hardly a problem came up in Europe during the next seventy years, nor has a solution been tried or found, which was not adumbrated in that year of intellectual fervour and political failure. But at first the storm seemed to have passed away, leaving the international frontiers of Europe exactly as they had been before; and even all the previous rulers, except in France, were restored, though no return was possible to the spirit of the preceding period or of its Governments. This perished in the Revolution of 1848. A time of "activism", reactionary or revolutionary, now ensued. In the course of the next thirty years the map of Europe was re-drawn, the initiative coming first from France, next from Prussia, and in the concluding years from Russia. The major problem of Central Europe was solved by the exclusion of the Habsburgs and of French influence from Germany and Italy; and a new form was given to the Habsburg possessions in the Dual Monarchy. Moreover, the problem of East-Central Europe was opened up by the partial disruption of Turkey, the weakest of the master nations; a line of independent States arose between Austria and Turkey which, with the backing of Russia, were to become a menace to both these non-national Empires.

This process was, however, arrested in 1878, and a new period of comparative rest supervened, with a reconstituted " Concert of Europe ". After another thirty-four years the problem of Turkey was reopened, followed closely by that of Austria-Hungary; and in the new cataclysm the small nations of East-Central Europe, from Finland to Greece, achieved their national unity, independence, and statehood. Poland arose through the defeat of Germany and Russia, not through her own effort or achievement. Driven by historical reminiscences and drawn by doubtful assets, she plunged into abysmal policies and insane adventures; and there was no Great Power to guide developments with a firm hand and purpose. For the position of France, who at Versailles seemed once more to preside over the destinies of Europe, had in the course of the century undergone a profound change.

IV

On the map of Europe the France of Versailles was practically identical with that of Vienna — slightly enlarged in the south by the inclusion of Savoy and

Nice, and holding exactly the same frontier against Germany as in 1815. But while at the beginning of the nineteenth century a coalition of almost all Europe was required to reduce France to that frontier, a hundred years later the Old World and the New had to combine in order to regain it for France. The frontier which had once been the mark of defeat now became the symbol of recovery, and while in 1815 international guarantees were devised against a possible recrudescence of French aggression, in 1919 they were sought to secure France against a fresh attack.

French predominance before 1815 was based on her superiority in numbers and organisation: on the relative size of her population and on the disunited condition of Germany and Italy. In 1815 France comprised about two-thirteenths of the population of Europe; in 1930, one-thirteenth. Barring Russia, enormous, inchoate, and distant, then as now protected and checked by her size, France in 1815 had of all the Great Powers the largest population — almost 30,000,000, against 26,000,000 in the heterogeneous, ill-assorted Austrian Empire, 13,000,000 in Great Britain (without Ireland), and 11,000,000 in Prussia. Since then France has received far more immigrants than she has sent out emigrants; while the 13,000,000 who inhabited Great Britain have probably now as many descendants in the United States and in the British Dominions and Colonies as in this island. But at present France takes numerically the seventh place among the Great Powers: Russia still comes first, followed by the United States, Japan, Germany, Great Britain, and Italy. All the *élan* of the Revolution and the genius of Napoleon could not have established French dominance over Europe had the proportion of numbers been then the same as now, and had the Germans and Italians been organised in united national States.

It was therefore in the interest of France, both before and after 1815, to preserve the territorial *status quo* in Germany and Italy. But the conquests of the French Revolution and Napoleon and the reactions to them, alike worked for the national consolidation of these countries. In 1789 Western and Central Germany was a collection of atomised principalities and free cities, with no one to hold an effective " Watch on the Rhine ". Napoleon did for Germany what none of her own princes could have done: he drastically reduced the number of German States, which never again exceeded forty. Similarly under Napoleon Italy approached unification. After 1815 the ideas of the French Revolution continued their work. The principle of national sovereignty and rights, overriding the prescriptive interests of the dynasties, pointed to national union. The programme of national union threatened the predominance of the Habsburgs in Germany and Italy, and the predominance of France in Europe. France and the Habsburgs had thus a common conservative interest. But national policy is seldom determined, in the long run, by calculation and thought; the greater the body the greater its inertia; States, like planets, move in predestined courses. France was set against Austria by an old rivalry based on the rules of political geography, by the social and ideological contrast which arose from the Revolution, and by the urge to action inherent in the Napoleonic tradition.

International alignments are usually based on the system of odd and even numbers. A common frontier between two independent States is as a rule a disputed frontier (unless it runs across the partitioned territory of a third nation, in which case the two States are neighbours, but not the two nations, which, moreover, combine to keep down the interposing third). " Les ennemis de mes ennemis sont mes amis " (neighbours quarrel; odds and evens are natural allies). This is the " sandwich system " of international politics. If, however, a State is composite and stratified (as was, for instance, Germany before 1870), there arises also a vertical series of numbers. In the sixteenth and seventeenth centuries the Habsburg emperors were opposed by the middle-sized, and supported by the small German States; France, therefore, in conflict with the Habsburgs, favoured the middle States. When Prussia under Frederick II entered the ranks of the Great Powers, European alignments were reversed in the so-called " Diplomatic Revolution ": Austria and France became allies. In 1815 it was their common interest to reconstitute that alliance. But under Metternich and his successors Austria remained suspicious of revolutionary France, while France, as in a dream, seemed to re-live the history of the Great Revolution and Napoleon.

Throughout the nineteenth century France was a " shell-shocked " nation — until 1870 by her own past greatness, after 1870 by her defeat. Like a man who, to overcome the effects of an overwhelming experience, continually reproduces it in his memory and emotions, so during the years 1815–1870 France re-lived the history of 1789–1815. The leading statesmen of those years were historians and supplied their own interpretations of the Revolution or the Empire: Guizot, Thiers, de Tocqueville, Lamartine, Louis Blanc, Falloux, Napoleon III, and many others. The great drama of the twenty-five revolutionary years was reproduced and attenuated in the slow-motion film of the fifty-five years 1815–1870. The opening attempt of the Revolution, to reconcile the *ancien régime* with modern ideas in a constitutional monarchy, was repeated under the Restoration. In the July Monarchy the bourgeoisie achieved the pre-eminence to which the *tiers état* had aspired in 1791. The Second Republic was consciously linked up with the Girondins, and it had its pseudo-Jacobins in the June Days, followed by a counter-revolutionary régime of disillusioned Republicans — like the Directory, bound to the Republic by their past, but no longer by faith. The Presidency of Louis Napoleon was a conscious repetition of the Consulate, and led up to the Second Empire. There was something singularly unreal and depressingly second-hand about this dream-play of French history, full of sadness, regrets, and scepticism, even during the apparent revival of national greatness. France had passed her zenith, without chance of return. But the past continued to dominate and predetermine the present. An alliance with Austria — support for the Habsburgs in Germany and Italy — was not in the records and traditions of the Revolution or the Empire. Far-seeing statesmen discerned the need of such a reorientation: the diplomats *de carrière* saw it, from Talleyrand to Drouyn de Lhuys, Guizot recognised it towards the end of his political career, and Thiers under the Second Empire. He wrote to Victor Cousin on May 10, 1866:

> ... the gain of two or three additional departments would be nothing compared with the misfortune of putting 50 million Germans into the hands of Prussia, and 25 million Italians into the hands of Piedmont. To further the growth of Prussia, to hasten the decline of Austria, is to commit irreparable blunders. ...

When, after Sadowa, France sought an alliance with Austria against Prussia, the Dual Monarchy, built on the German-Magyar basis, was no longer able to respond.

The defeat of 1870 awakened France. It was the bankruptcy of the heroic legends: that of the Empire perished at Sedan, that of the Revolution in Gambetta's failure — the magic slogans of *la patrie en danger* and *levée en masse* had proved ineffective. France, after eighty years of dreams and fever, was seeking a way back to reality, to a routine of life. In international affairs she wished for security, or at the most for reparation, no longer for predominance. The Franco-Russian alliance was formed against the Central Powers, to restore the balance in Europe. In the Berlin-Baghdad programme and in naval armaments Germany was transcending the European arena; but in 1912–1913 the disruption of European Turkey, affecting and infecting Austria-Hungary, reopened European problems — the problem of the submerged nationalities of East-Central

Europe. War between Russia and the two Germanic Powers unrolled the Polish Question. The nineteenth century was drawing to its logical close.

In 1914 two solutions of the Polish Question held the field: the programme of the "Austrian Solution", a union of Austrian and Russian Poland under the Habsburgs, possibly including some White Russian and Ukrainian territory, but without Prussian Poland; the other was that of a complete ethnic reunion of all undoubtedly Polish lands, Russian, Austrian, and Prussian, in conjunction with Russia. What actually happened no one could have foreseen: there remained not one victorious Great Power in Eastern Europe. The Habsburg Monarchy disappeared, and Poland arose in a void, at the expense both of Germany and Russia. But a nation of twenty-odd millions cannot permanently form a barrier between one of one hundred and fifty and another of seventy-five millions, hostile to both. In 1919, in the series of odd and even numbers, France obtained for partners Poland and the Little Entente; Italy and Russia were left to Germany. Each of the four Succession States allied to France was of mixed nationality, and each therefore was in a precarious situation. Largely through the fault of Poland, in the first serious crisis they failed to stand together; nor did France evince the necessary strength and determination to uphold the system which she had created.

The "Vienna to Versailles" period has run its course. Whatever the weaknesses may have been of the system created in 1919, a return to previous forms is impossible. They have been broken, and broken for good. The rule of dynasties and the imperialisms of "master nations" are dead. The ethnic basis has been postulated for States, and if violated it will be violated with the ferocious brutality of the Nazis. The criterion of nationality was adopted in 1919, but was not pressed to its logical conclusion. Transfers of population carried through in a sensible manner will have to form the basis of future arrangements. If the national singleness of the migrating hordes is to be regained, hordes will have to migrate once more. The first task is to save Europe from the Nazi onslaught — a difficult task; but even greater will be the work of resettling a morally and materially bankrupt world on a new basis.

AFTER VIENNA AND VERSAILLES

("*The Nineteenth Century and After*", November 1940)

I

WHY was France never able to call in question the bases of the Vienna settlement of 1815, and what was it that has enabled Germany, only twenty years after her defeat, to challenge and destroy the Treaties concluded at the end of the last war?

There was harmony and integration in the origin, course, and outcome of the wars of 1792–1815. The settlement reached at Vienna in 1815, in spite of previous discord among the Allies, satisfied the four Great Powers which had fought and vanquished Napoleon; they were its chief beneficiaries and had an interest in preserving it. The Quadruple Alliance continued a latent existence for at least one generation.

There was incongruity and paradox in the origin, course, and outcome of the war of 1914–1918. Of the six Great Powers which fought Imperial Germany, Russia became a victim in the final settlement, Italy and Japan were estranged, the United States withdrew from European affairs in disgust, and Great Britain, repeatedly flouted in Eastern Europe, tried to restrict her responsibilities to the West. France was left with the victory and its European progeny upon her hands. That progeny, in its " living space " between Germany,

Italy, and Russia, comprised thirteen states — new, much enlarged, or severely truncated — with over a hundred million inhabitants, more than a score of disputed frontiers, and some fifty burning problems. The three World Powers — the United States, the British Empire, and Russia — had no positive interest in upholding the territorial settlement established in that region; and the Coalition of the War of 1914–1918 was dead before the Peace Treaties were concluded.

The French Revolution had challenged the social and political order of Europe, which still comprised virtually the whole civilised world of the white race. Predominance on the European Continent, then even more than now, pointed to world-dominion, especially when coupled with an aggressive, revolutionary creed. Great Britain and Russia were the gates through which Napoleon had to break if he was to reach the vast extra-European spaces. Still, even these Powers, on the two flanks of the European Continent, fought him as Europeans, in a European Coalition, over European problems.

The war of 1914 was again European in its immediate causes and in its consequences; yet its origin and outcome were largely conditioned by extra-European problems and forces. Had it not been for Germany's world-wide ambitions and the resulting conflict with the Anglo-Saxon Powers, the war, which turned on a stage in the logical advance of European nationalisms, would either not have broken out or would soon have ended in a German victory. The intervention of the Anglo-Saxon Powers and the defeat of Germany, coupled with the collapse of Russia, cleared the ground for the rise of the small nations in the European Middle East to independent state existence; but this was a development in which Britain and America had no immediate interest, and for which neither would have gone to war. Moreover, a superiority of France over Germany was re-established such as France herself had no longer hoped for or aimed at. Here were two logical consequences of an incongruous situation.

II

Germany's primacy on the European Continent had been established by Bismarck's victories, and secured through the wise restraint of his policy during the next twenty years. Whereas the French Revolution and Napoleon had from the very outset challenged England and Russia, Bismarck was careful not to drive either into active hostility; and as long as these two Powers could safely acquiesce in Germany's predominance in the centre of Europe, there was no one on that Continent sufficient to dispute it. The Habsburg Monarchy had been reconstructed on a German-Magyar basis, which both fitted and forced it into the German system; France was isolated and immobilised. For centuries Vienna and Paris had been the centres of European power-politics: now Berlin overshadowed them, and its pre-eminence grew steadily through the prodigious increase in Germany's population and resources.

By the end of the nineteenth century, the programme of *revanche* had paled into a theoretical hope, remembered but not contemplated. In the Boulanger crisis, France had passed through, and had overcome, the paroxysm of pathological nationalism which invariably sets in about fifteen years after a major defeat.[1] Almost every theory, delusion, or trick in the Nazi repertory finds its remarkable, though less vile and brutal, counterpart in the demagogical militarist and anti-Semitic movements which centred round Boulanger, Déroulède, and Drumont; there was the same nationalist exasperation and effervescence, a similar mixture of radicalism and reaction, the same reviling of the Parliamentary Republic, of its sins and " corruption ", the same hysterical adulation of an individual before he had any achievements to his credit: but resistance at home and obstacles abroad prevented the emotions behind the Boulanger movement from ever being translated into practice. Meanwhile a generation grew up no longer beset by the poignant memories of 1870; and the Russian alliance, though it created a better feeling of security, disappointed those who had pinned on it hopes of *revanche*. The passionate dream of the preceding generation was fading. " *La fin du siècle* " in France was a period of dramatic internal contests, of cultural endeavour, moral elevation, and of high intellectual achievement. Conscious pacifism was gaining ground, and — the clearest evidence of strength — it found expression in two otherwise antagonistic movements: the French labour movement, under its great leader Jaurès, hoped and strove for international reconciliation through the working classes, while important sections of the propertied classes, represented by men like Rouvier and Caillaux, looked to

[1] Cf. essay on " Pathological Nationalisms " in my book *In the Margin of History*.

international co-operation of a financial character.

But the dictum of Napoleon III — " When France is contented, Europe is at peace " — no longer held good after 1870. And now William II's ill-defined world ambitions and confused world-politics supplied a new background to the European scene. He would suffer no limitation to his claims to be heard, or to the weight of his armaments. He menaced England and estranged Russia. At times he attempted a Continental bloc against England — during the Boer War and at Björkoe — in which France was to play the satellite and accomplice of German *Weltpolitik*. But if there was to be no reversal of 1870, France meant at least to preserve her dignity and independence. Feelings of uncertainty and unrest evoked by German strength and bluster produced the Anglo-French Entente, originally a move towards political preparedness, not an alliance. The English had an engrained aversion to Continental commitments; the French had even better reason to move warily. For the Germans, blackmailers to the core, were announcing with glee that should England prove beyond their reach, France, if her ally, was to make up for it as " hostage " and prey; and the French knew what a war with Germany might entail for them in suffering and losses. Twice after the Entente had been formed, in the Morocco crises of 1905-6 and 1911, France, though assured of British assistance, preferred to placate the Germans; and Russia had to give way to them in the Bosnian crisis of 1909. These were withdrawals, not capitulations, though Germany tried to render them humiliating, so as to obtain from them the fullest enjoyment, and perhaps also in order to discredit the Entente. Actually Germany's conduct produced a hardening of British resistance and a growth of nationalist feeling in Russia and France. Two men came to the fore who remembered 1870, actually and politically, Poincaré and Clemenceau.

British support had to be given if France and Russia were to be enabled to stand up to Germany; or else they might have been forced into the German orbit and into a partnership directed against this country. This support the Germans described as a policy of " incitement ", " encirclement ", and of making those countries fight Britain's battles (but, in fact, Russia and France entered the war in 1914 before they were perfectly certain of Britain's active support). No one in this country will say that America is inciting us because her aid helps us to fight a battle which she knows is ultimately her battle. Nor would German fudge and fustian deserve a reply. But in the bitterness of defeat misapprehensions are apt to arise in the French mind. A decline in the French *élan* was noticeable during the period 1890–1910; and the revival in French nationalism and action occurred against the background of the Anglo-German conflict. The chance which this offered roused the French to one supreme last effort, and the victory of 1918 carried them further than their Anglo-Saxon friends ever wished them to go. There followed ebullition, failure, and decline; torpor, a convulsion, and agony.

AFTER VIENNA AND VERSAILLES

III

In the break-up of European Turkey, 1912–1913, the process of national re-formation was resumed which, after thirty active years, had been arrested in 1878. The expulsion of the Turks from the Balkans had always been an aim of Russian Greek-Orthodoxy and Pan-Slavism. It also lay in the logic of European development, to be followed by the disruption of the Habsburg Monarchy. This, too, was in Russia's Greek-Orthodox, Pan-Slav programme; but it had never been an aim of British, nor of French policy. Still, when the problem of the subject nationalities of Austria-Hungary moved into the foreground and, in the conflict which ensued, her continued existence became the touchstone of German superiority over the European Continent, Britain could not remain indifferent to the power problem, even though she had no immediate interest in the territorial issues. At the root of the war of 1914 lay a Russian interest, sentiment, and tradition. The war ended without Russia, and the process which she had fostered was concluded at her own expense. The development was logical but absurd. For if a new order was to be secured in East-Central Europe it could not be against all the Great Powers east of the Rhine. Russia's collapse left a void and a burden which from the outset vitiated the peace settlement. This was still further complicated by the French system of alliances, the Anglo-Saxon delusion of a League of Nations, and the universal horror of Bolshevism.

France had lost more than 1,500,000 dead in a war

which had not been of her initiative or making: a terrible loss for a nation stationary, or even declining, in numbers. What she now craved was security, foremost perhaps the assurance of never again having to wage such a war, or make such sacrifices. Her system of alliances in East-Central Europe was as imperfect and as deceptive as her Maginot Line later on: and both belonged to the same order of thought and were to have served the same purpose. But fear and an anxious economy cramp the human spirit, and deprive both policy and strategy of the necessary balance, *élan*, and freedom. The progeny of victory was to have sustained its parent; but it gradually dawned on the French that their system, which attracted the hostility of three Great Powers, besides two small ones, was a liability rather than an asset.[1] They tried to bolster it up by recourse to League ideas: which, in turn, landed them in new difficulties. And after having been imperious and rash, they finished by becoming distracted and listless. Political juggling cannot do away with numbers, weights, and measures, nor do sermons and signatures transform human nature. No system can be permanently maintained on the European Continent east of the Rhine, which has not the support either of Germany or of Russia, especially if its other guarantors are not anxious to exert themselves.

[1] Cf. the essay on "French Policy in Europe, 1919–1938" in my book *In the Margin of History*.

IV

The League of Nations was essentially an Anglo-Saxon idea; it was the continuation, or rather the revival, in the sphere of international politics, of the faith, the facile optimism and comfortable illusions, of mid-nineteenth century "utilitarian" believers in democracy. These were based on the triple conviction that the pursuit of the good was a matter of right reasoning, that right reasoning was a matter of education, and that whoever thought rightly would act rightly; moreover, that peace was the "normal" condition of humanity, and any deviation from it was a lapse from grace.[1] In the prosperous, self-satisfied atmosphere of America, mid-Victorian ideas survived into the twentieth century, and at the end of the Great War, Woodrow Wilson, "impassioned admirer of Bright and Gladstone, transplanted the nineteenth century rationalist faith to the almost virgin soil of international politics, and, bringing it back with him to Europe, gave it a new lease of life".[2] When on his way to Paris he was asked "by some of his advisers whether he thought his plan of a League of Nations would work, he replied briefly: ' If it won't work, it must be made to work ' ".[3]

Did President Wilson realise what supreme exertions this would have entailed? The "Pax Anglo-Saxonica", to be effective, required an Anglo-Saxon world police; in fact, a world dominion exercised by

[1] On the mid-Victorian origin of the League idea, see Professor E. H. Carr's brilliant book, *The Twenty Years' Crisis.*
[2] *Ibid.* p. 37.   [3] *Ibid.* p. 12.

America and the British Empire. But was either prepared for such an undertaking? Even at the Peace Conference it was difficult enough to obtain right decisions. The Anglo-Saxon Powers, being uninterested, tended to be just; France tried to please and oblige her numerous and clamorous *clientèle*; Italy was keen on misdrawing frontiers, each violation of the principle of nationality constituting a precedent for her own preposterous demands; and as for Japan, one of her representatives, when asked to decide in a tie between the two Anglo-Saxon and the two Latin Powers, significantly replied that " the Japanese delegation voted with the majority ". Long before the close of the Peace Conference, the effective control of affairs had slipped from the hands of the Anglo-Saxon Powers, as it was only too obvious that in neither country would public opinion have suffered the sending of troops to enforce a decision however just, or to prevent an outrage however flagrant, in regions in which they were not interested. The defeated Great Powers — Russia and Germany — were prostrate, and the victorious Great Powers became silent, loth to contend where unable to determine. In this void, small nations staked out and imposed their claims and, with little share in the victory, became its chief and inordinate beneficiaries. Such was the paradoxical and incongruous outcome of the War of 1914–1918: was the League to guarantee or to correct the settlement?

Too clear an answer to this question would have meant trouble. The League was to cure humanity and lead it into better ways. It was an expression of the morality and idealism of the Anglo-Saxons, and of their ignorance of what it means to suffer of neighbours and disputed borderlands (Ulster alone knows it). The alchemists set out with the belief that there must be a way of making gold, because they had the will to make it. The Anglo-Saxons wanted peace; to show up the impossibilities of the League nostrum was considered " destructive and unhelpful " — for " what will you put in its place? " Insularity, not internationalism, was the life-breath of the League idea. Besides, there was shrewdness and self-deception, the will to do good and the wish to have it cheap; a vast amount of humane feeling, confused thinking, and doctrinaire impatience.

The Anglo-Saxon mind, like the Jewish, is inclined to legalism. In the eighteenth century the problem of American taxation was discussed in the British Parliament in terms of law, precedent, and custom. It was then that Great Britain learnt the futility of such methods. America, in isolation and under a federal system, has preserved a good deal of the legalistic outlook. In the Covenant, President Wilson gave the League of Nations a written constitution, but without the moral basis of true acceptance or the backing of force — the burden of legalism without the advantages of law. Tsarist Russia led the Entente into war in 1914 and collapsed before its close; President Wilson founded the League and was disavowed by America: Great Britain had first to go through with the War, and next with the League.

In the 1850's Bismarck declared that if Prussia was to be fixed in loyalty to the " German idea " and hostility against France, there was no room for a foreign policy.

AFTER VIENNA AND VERSAILLES

After 1919 England tied herself up in loyalty to the "League idea" and hostility to Bolshevik Russia: henceforth Great Britain had no foreign policy. With the great mass of the British public, in that "League idea" peace counted for more than justice, and disarmament for more than "collective security". Moreover — "what is justice?" Whenever legal obligations encounter a passionate aversion to danger and action, feeble subterfuges and self-defeating compromises are resorted to: for instance, sanctions are imposed but not pressed to a point at which, by becoming effective, they might provoke war. Mr. Wickham Steed, an expert on international politics and a champion of the League, writes in his book on *Our War Aims*: "If we meant to turn our backs on a League policy of collective security against war, we ought to have re-armed much sooner". But would it not be truer to say that we ought to have done so if we meant to stand by collective security? For surely Japan, Italy, and Germany could be expected to start with China, Abyssinia, Austria, and Czechoslovakia, rather than with Great Britain. League of Nations principles, seriously held, are incompatible with the blind, unconditional pacifism which swelled the following of the League idea and was (perhaps against the wish of the leaders) stimulated by League propaganda. Hitler, after each performance, had merely to talk of rejoining the League or of signing some new "Non-Aggression Pact" for enthusiastic pacifists to proclaim that to doubt his sincerity would be a crime.

V

Some people Hitler could best reassure by talking about peace, others by inveighing against the " Reds ". It was, of course, against these, and against no one else, that he was arming!

In 1815 France, under the Bourbon Restoration, received remarkably lenient treatment: could anyone visit the crimes of the Revolution and Napoleon on these illustrious sufferers? They were Europe's first line of defence against a recurrence of war, against Jacobins and Bonapartists — " with the Bourbons, war was neither a need nor a passion ". They could claim, and received, consideration.

In 1918 the Germans tried their transformation trick: the Weimar Republic would " render the world safe for democracy ". But were Socialists and Democrats a safe line of defence against Bolshevism? By 1919 Europe feared the " Reds " more than the Kaiser. The Weimar Republic aroused no enthusiasm and received little consideration.

Fifteen years after 1815 the July Revolution overthrew the Bourbons. In 1830 and 1840, fear of French aggression, an aggression tinged with revolution, drew the European Powers closer together. Napoleon III had to talk *Realpolitik* to reassure Europe.

Fifteen years after 1918 the Nazis overthrew the Weimar Republic. Blood was spilt, but the blood of " Reds "; atrocities were committed, but the excuses offered had a counter-revolutionary colouring. In every country there were people eager to find evidence of the good which Hitler was supposed to have done to his country: he has "saved Germany from Communism"; "restored her self-respect"; the Jews — well, "they are not without blame"; the atrocities are "exaggerated"; the Versailles Treaty was "harsh".

1830 lost for France the indulgence accorded to the Bourbons; 1933 won for Germany the indulgence withheld from the Weimar Republic. Would M. Laval and M. Daladier, Mr. Baldwin and Mr. Chamberlain, have been so slow in sensing danger had a Bolshevik Germany re-armed on such a scale?

VI

Without Russia no stable system can be established on the European Continent to keep Germany in check. Under pressure of the present war the English-speaking nations are drawing closer together and developing a powerful extra-European system of defence, of which Great Britain is the advanced European bastion. In the days when naval superiority was sufficient to ensure the safety of the British Isles, the shores facing them were our frontier and the sea was our line of defence. Now that line must include the aerodromes along those shores. Norway, Denmark, and the Low Countries have learnt that there is no such thing as "neutrality" in relations with Germany. They and France are essential to the Anglo-Saxon defensive system. But France will no longer be able to play the rôle of "*puissance protectrice*" in East-Central Europe. As such she failed whenever she was faced by German-Russian co-operation — in the eighteenth century, when she was unable to protect Sweden, Poland, and

Turkey; in the nineteenth century, when she failed effectively to help Poland; in the twentieth century, at Munich, at the siege of Warsaw, and at Vichy. But will, or could, even the Anglo-Saxon Powers undertake such a task? With Europe east of the Rhine left to itself, there can be Anglo-Saxon armed security, but there can be no real peace; only co-operation between the English-speaking nations and Russia can regain for Europe the stability which, at the end of the last war, was compromised by the virtual withdrawal of the three World Empires. Those smaller nations which, after 1919, wished and worked for the isolation and proscription of Russia, must now realise what chances this has given to the Germans who, united as they never were before, will remain a danger to Europe unless a firm ring is formed around them.

THE GERMAN INTERNATIONAL

("*The Nineteenth Century and After*", May 1940)

[This essay brings an unfinished story up to April 1940, before the Germans overran Western and South-Eastern Europe. Its character has not changed, but the plot has thickened. I have not altered the story, not even its tenses.]

I

THE most effective, and yet as a rule the least impugned, "International" has been that of the Germans. A hundred years ago, it was the International of the dynasties, now it is of the German "*Volksgemeinschaft*". In 1840 the ruling families of all the Great Powers, except France, and of most of the smaller countries, were in essence German, and there were many scores of dynasties in Germany, ruling or *quondam* sovereign, anxious to supply brides or candidates for any and every throne. In fact, the German guild of princes had managed to impose on Europe a German "racial" theory, utterly alien to the traditions of most other nations, about the blood of sovereigns having to be "uncontaminated" by that of non-princely families. Even for the eldest son of Louis-Philippe the bride had to be sought and found in what Bismarck, on a later occasion, coarsely described as "the German stud". Nor could a new throne be raised anywhere from Mexico to Bulgaria, or an old one fall vacant, without a Coburg, a Habsburg, a Wittelsbach, or a Hohenzollern coming forward as candidate. The last, rather farcical, swarming of German princes occurred during the years 1913–1918: the Prince of Wied in Albania, Austrian Archdukes as candidates for the thrones of Poland and the Ukraine, the Duke of Urach aspiring to become " Mindowe II " of Lithuania, Friedrich Karl of Hesse as candidate for the Finnish throne, etc. A legend has been fostered of a German cosmopolitanism in the first part of the nineteenth century, a " *Weltbürgertum* ", a " universality " tinged with renunciation, when rather it was the case of an International based on the ubiquity of German dynasties, at a time when dynastic power was a reality.

That chapter is now closed for ever. But in the " *Volksgenossen* " it has left a heritage to the new phase of German influence. German permeation and colonisation were furthered and encouraged by the princes. The Habsburgs did a great deal to Germanise their Czech and Slovene provinces, and planted German colonies in the Bukovina, the Carpathian Mountains, the Banat, Slavonia, etc. Catherine II (of Anhalt-Zerbst) and her successors settled German villages on the Volga, in Southern Russia, and in Bessarabia. And even in the original German migrations to Pennsylvania and Georgia, the Hanoverian connexion was not without influence. There is no other nation possessing a State of its own which is so widely scattered as the German. They form important and coherent colonies in most trans-oceanic countries, and, barring four countries on the circumference (Finland, Albania, Greece, and Bulgaria), there was in 1933 no State in Central and Eastern Europe, hardly even a Soviet republic, which did not harbour a German minority.

While politics were mainly dynastic and most dynasties were German, these minorities, though often obnoxious or even oppressive to their neighbours, did not profess allegiance to an extraneous Power, and were therefore not alien or hostile to the State. The rise of the Hohenzollern Empire in 1871 produced a new Pan-Germanism, at first held in check by Bismarck's realist genius, but subsequently stimulated by William II's unbalanced braggadocio. There was fervour and bombast in the Second Reich, mental indigestion and great efficiency. They talked "*Urgeschichte*", Nordic trash, and Nietzschean a-morality, and they built up the most powerful modern industry and army. They prided themselves on their barbaric past, as no other nation ever did, and their actions were yet to bear witness both to that past and their pride in it. At the same time they claimed to be "*ein Herrenvolk*" with a mission as "*Kulturträger*": the scattered German minorities were changing into conscious outposts of an aggressive creed. German trade combined with German politics, and both were carried into the world by emissaries from the Reich working with, on, and through long-established minorities. In Austria the Pan-Germans, led by politicians from the Sudetenland, demanded a new and sharper "*Kurs*" (policy). The Habsburg dynasty, the Roman Catholic Church, and the Austrian Army Command, had done far more than the Hohenzollerns to spread "*Deutschtum*" in East-Central and South-Eastern Europe; but they had learnt that dominion to be far-flung has to be at least tolerable. Such a system did not satisfy the Pan-German secondary-school teacher and the petty middle-class intelligentsia who aspired to power over their non-German neighbours: where there is to be a vast number of citizen rulers, there must be a slave population. Young Hitler dreamt the turgid Pan-German dreams, resented the inferiority of his father who was a small Austrian official, was determined not to become one himself, and transferred the dislike and contempt which he felt for his father on to the Habsburgs, whose uniform and rosette his father wore. To him, as to others, the Hohenzollerns were the symbol of a victorious, virile, ruthless Germanism. In 1897 the Pan-Germans, when accused by the Austrian Premier, Count Badeni, a Pole, of "squinting" into the Reich, replied by a song which was sung in the streets of Vienna:

> "Wir schielen nicht, wir schauen,
> Wir schauen unverwandt,
> Wir schauen voll Vertrauen,
> Ins deutsche Vaterland".[1]

On a later occasion when, at the end of a debate on the Address in the Vienna Parliament, the customary cheers were to be raised for the Austrian Emperor, the leader of the Bohemian Pan-Germans called out: "*Ein Hoch und Heil dem Hause Hohenzollern*".

Thirty-three years ago I heard at Lausanne University of a German lecturer who, referring to the French character of the place, exhorted a meeting of German students, his compatriots from the Reich: "*Meine*

[1] "We do not squint, we look,
We look and do not falter,
We look with full reliance,
Into the German Fatherland."

Herren, gedenket immer, Ihr seid hier in Feindesland".[1] (Incidentally, none of these students wearing " German colours " could have risked, even at that time, to be seen in company with a Jew, and they were highly indignant when they discovered that a man of Jewish origin had joined them in getting drunk on " the Kaiser's birthday ".) The essentials of Hitlerism were being developed by the pre-1914 generation, and throughout the world the Germans were already flaunting their " *Deutschtum* " with a provocative arrogance such as only a rare combination of " *Machtbewusstsein* " (consciousness of power) and bad taste can produce. In spite of the widely different antecedents of the two men, William II was an unmistakable forerunner of Hitler, and the uncanny parallelism between them shows that they both truly voice the same element in Germany's national development and spirit.

What a victory of the Central Powers would have meant east of the Rhine was clearly indicated in the programmes of *Mitteleuropa* and Berlin-Baghdad, and in the peace treaties of Brest-Litovsk and Bucharest. Defeat swept away the Habsburg Monarchy and the compromise for which it stood — of a dominant, nonnationalistic Germanism. The capital of Russia had been removed to Moscow, and St. Petersburg had changed its name and lost its German dynasty and its Baltic barons. With the death of Carol I of Rumania and the flight of Ferdinand of Bulgaria, dynastic German influence ceased to predominate in Bucharest and Sofia. Wherever the Germans were a minority in Central and Eastern Europe, they were now a minority

[1] " Gentlemen, always bear in mind that you are here in enemy country."

like any other — no longer a pampered or dominant minority — and they had to yield first place to the "majority" nation. Help or protection could not come to them any more from German princes; and there were no princes left in Germany. Loyalties to old States and dynasties had broken down, and the slight veneer of tradition embodied in the upper classes had disappeared. There was everywhere a clash of the nationalisms of the masses; the levelling, lowering influence of the last war had created a void; Hitler stepped into it with his "*Volkstum*", the "*Volksgemeinschaft*" of all the German "*Volksgenossen*", wherever they have been born and of whatever State they are citizens — an ominous message for any community harbouring a German minority.

II

German influence, powerfully operating at the centre, had permeated the Habsburg Monarchy and infected Tsarist Russia; yet the size of these Empires had been also a check on Germany. Now the map had been re-drawn against Germany; still, east and south-east of her, there was no State fit to offset the weight, political, military, and economic, inherent in her numbers and organisation. Even in the 1920's there were doubts about the stability of the French system, which was based on Poland and the Little Entente: hence the eager quest after the Geneva Protocol. The economic crisis, which opened in 1929, began an era in European history and supplied a dangerous background for the flourishes of a Mussolini, the fumblings of a

Ramsay MacDonald, and the perplexities of French foreign policy. The depression affected the widest masses even in the remotest countries, produced " a crystallisation of disappointments and prejudices ", hardened " intolerance all the world over ",[1] and everywhere brought new political forces to the surface, violent and brutal — National Socialists and National Radicals, " patriotic fronts " and an " Iron Guard ". The " Awakening Magyars " and the Italian Fascists had been forerunners of such movements; Hitler's victory made Germany their focus and model. The new totalitarian, dictatorial, anti-Semitic International found in every country its reflection, and in every German minority its transmitters: the response of the " *Auslandsdeutschen* " (Germans outside Germany), and especially of their youth, shows how deeply Nazism is rooted in the German character and instincts.

In international relations totalitarian systems have certain marked advantages over freer forms of Government: there is no possibility of effective opposition under dictatorships, whereas the freedom of political life in non-totalitarian States enables Nazis and pro-Nazis to impede the work and undermine the position of those whom they mean to destroy. Colonel Beck and M. Stoyadinovich could pursue their fatal policy of collaboration with Hitler, unchecked by the intense dislike which the vast majority of Poles and Yugoslavs felt for it; while in democratic countries reactionary groups could freely favour the dictators and work for the destruction of Republican Spain and Czecho-

---

[1] Elizabeth Wiskemann, *Undeclared War* (Constable, 12s.). Further quotations in this chapter, unless marked otherwise, are all from that book.

slovakia. Another advantage results from the absolute control which dictatorships exercise over the economic system and transactions of their countries; a third, from the ease with which a political *volte-face* can be accomplished; a fourth, from the unmeasured, freely flaunted brutality of these professional thugs, which intimidates and, like the boa constrictor, fascinates " rabbits " among the leaders and the public.

The Austrian *Anschluss* does not enter into the purview of this essay, which deals with the technique of the German International based on German minorities; nor does even the story of how Czechoslovakia was thrown to the wolves when there was " Peace with Honour " — the diplomacy and statesmanship of the appeasers destroyed a State which the Nazis had not been able to suborn or to infect, and a country over which they had failed to obtain economic ascendancy. It is in Hungary, Rumania, Yugoslavia, and Poland (before 1939) that the " Undeclared War " of the Nazis can best be studied; and the work of analysing their methods has been brilliantly done by Miss Wiskemann in the book on which the following pages are based.

Cn a moderate estimate the German minority amounted in 1939 to 600,000 in Hungary; 600,000 in Yugoslavia; 750,000 in Rumania; and in Poland it was also about 750,000: a field for Nazi propagandist and organising activities. Hungary had provinces to reclaim; Rumania, Yugoslavia, and Poland to retain: a field for Nazi intrigue. There were 3,300,000 Jews in Poland, and there are 800,000 in Rumania and 500,000 in Hungary; outside Germany these are the three most anti-Semitic countries in the world: a happy field for Nazi racial doctrines. Truncated Hungary was as difficult to reorganise and govern as were the tasselated Succession States: a hungry, half-baked intelligentsia, rabid with nationalism, politics, and ambitions, and corroded with the disillusionment of the post-war period, offered in these four countries rich seed plots for would-be dictators. The collapse of the markets for agricultural produce created a catastrophic position in these four great food-producing countries: Germany was the only important buyer, eager to take their unsaleable goods, but on terms and under a system which were to give her a stranglehold on the life of these countries.

Since 1919 the demand for treaty revision dominated the thoughts and policy of the Magyars: theirs was a constant and indefatigable search for allies to effect such revision.

> In 1932, just before Hitler came to power, General Gömbös became Prime Minister of Hungary. This man, like a considerable number of Hungarians, was half German by descent and almost Nazi in outlook, and from 1933 Nazi propaganda from Germany, countenanced by him and his protégés playing upon so many Magyar prejudices, made great strides.

As the military strength of the Nazis and their political *élan* developed, the Magyars felt that here at last was a chance of realising their national dream. Also personal interests worked in favour of the Nazis:

> ... from the time of Austria's fall, if not even

earlier, bureaucrats and important police officials and even one or two highly placed members of the judiciary seemed to be preparing, like many other Austrian officials before them, to stand on the right side of Hitler; they intended to be safe from dismissals or reprisals should any kind of Nazi régime — German or dependent upon Germany — be installed at Budapest.

At the general election of May 1938 — two months after the *Anschluss* — the Hungarian Nazis, with financial and moral support from Germany, increased their representation from five or six to forty-three seats; while " perhaps half the Government Party itself sympathised actively with the Nazis ". When Czecho-slovakia was partitioned in the autumn of 1938, the Magyars effected their first recovery of territory lost in 1918–1919: they obtained a broad strip of country inhabited by Magyars and Slovaks along their north-eastern border; and when in March 1939 the Nazis entered Prague, the Magyars seized Carpatho-Russia and another slice of Slovakia.

Nazi successes are Hungary's chance, but also Hungary's danger. With Austria incorporated in Germany, the Burgenland, one of Hungary's lost provinces, will be German so long as the Nazis remain supreme. If Nazi dominion over the Czechs has given the Magyars one part of Slovakia, it has placed the rest under a German protectorate. Nor is it pleasing or safe for Hungary, containing a German minority of 600,000, to have so long a frontier with Germany and her Slovak protectorate. The Magyars are in danger of becoming German janissaries, " *eine gleichgeschaltete Hilfsmacht* "

They hope for further conquests and fear the price which they will be made to pay.

The Magyar Nazis advocating wholeheartedly " extreme anti-Semitism and uncompromising dictatorship " are in a minority, especially among the upper classes which are imbued with an old political and parliamentary tradition. But they have a fairly numerous popular following and a chance to gain a much larger. They have taken up the cry for land reform against the Conservative land-owning aristocracy; rampant anti-Semitism helps them with the intelligentsia and the lower middle class; and even among the working classes they seem to have made considerable progress. Altogether they appeal to " the young and destitute ".

The German minority, which before the advent of the Nazis, in spite of a steady curtailment of their educational and cultural rights, professed fervent loyalty to the Hungarian Government, has assumed a different tone since 1933, and still more since 1938. They are now openly taught, and have accepted, the doctrine that their allegiance is primarily due to Hitler, the leader of the race, and that it is the mission of the Germans to rule over other, inferior, races. Their demand for German schools in Hungary is pressed with marked success, and it is feared that " a growing number of apparently assimilated Hungarians of German descent may wish to revert to the Germanism which nowadays involves the possibility of privilege ". Dr. Basch himself, elected in December 1938 President of the Nazi *Volksbund der Deutschen in Ungarn*, " was once a Hungarian Chauvinist ". In the General Election of 1938, with the connivance of the Hungarian Government, pressure was exerted on the Hungarian Germans to vote for the Nazi candidates: these secured about two-thirds of their votes.

Meantime the Hungarian Government, both in order to please and to check the Nazis, has adopted parts of their programme, foremost in the matter of anti-Jewish restrictions. The Prime Minister who introduced the legislation, M. Imredy, is himself of German descent (but when it was proved against him that he has also some Jewish blood he had to resign). Ousting the Jews helps the German economic conquest of Hungary. Most of her industries and trade was developed and worked by the Jews; of roughly 3000 factories about 1500, including all the major concerns, were in their hands. There are not Magyars fit or even available to fill the place of all the Jews who are to be displaced, and consequently jobs and business will pass into the hands, or under the control, of the Germans. It is the Nazi aim in Hungary, Rumania, and Yugoslavia to render the economy of these countries subservient and complementary to that of Germany: they are to specialise in the production of food and raw materials required by Germany, but to engage in industry only where it is of a non-competing character.

A few years ago, when there was a glut in raw materials, the Germans started by offering Hungary, Rumania, and Yugoslavia inflated prices for their produce, and thus raised the price levels of these countries. Since then the Nazis have forced them to accept an artificially low rate of exchange between their own currencies and German marks. In other words, while the prices are inflated when measured in terms of free currencies, the Germans pay for their own purchases at cut rates. Lastly, the conquest of Austria and Czechoslovakia has completed the German hold over the three other Succession States. Austria has always been a good market for Hungarian, Rumanian, and Yugoslav agricultural produce and supplied these countries with foreign exchange. Since March 1938 trade with Austria is only another form of trade with Germany. Czechoslovakia, too, was a good market for these States, controlled some of their industries, and was the chief supplier of armaments for Rumania and Yugoslavia. The conquest of Czechoslovakia has given the Nazis control of a number of Yugoslav industries, and in the matter of armaments a stranglehold both over Yugoslavia and Rumania.

In Rumania the main opponents of the Nazi creed and of a pro-German policy are the notorious " Iron Guard ", a Rumanian version of a quasi-mystical " *Volkstum* ". The " racial " game, however, was spoilt a little by the fact that their leader, Zelea Codreanu, alias Zielinski, " a young man of romantic appearance ", was not of Rumanian, but of Polish extraction, with an admixture of German or even Hungarian blood (similarly in the case of Major Szálasi, the leader of the Magyar Nazis, the enthusiasm for Magyar racial purity " was impaired by the discovery of his own mixed Armenian-Slovak-German descent "). The Iron Guard, which was indebted to Germany for much of its income and of its revolutionary *élan*, indulged in the extremest forms of anti-Semitism, demanded a complete dictatorship with a social revolutionary programme, and both threatened and practised assassination. They also demanded the merciless assimilation of minorities in Rumania: and none the less had the active support of the German Nazis, sensitive to real or alleged sufferings of German minorities only when it suits their game.

Governing circles in Rumania, even when opposed to the Iron Guard, often display the " hypnotised rabbit " condition. In various ways they show favour to the Iron Guard, while trying to get away with some of its popularity and programme. One anti-Semitic measure after another is introduced in Rumania, and in between the assassination of ministers by the Iron Guard and the killing of Iron Guards " while trying to escape ", the Government blows hot and cold on them, and endeavours to capture their following. It tries to attract young people by the " dazzlingly blue uniforms " of the " Front of National Re-birth ", complete with Fascist salutations and " Sanatate ", the Rumanian equivalent for the Nazi " Heil ".

Meantime in Rumania, as in Hungary, the German minority is being drawn or forced into the Nazi organisation. The Transylvanian Saxons, who always felt a racial superiority over the Rumanians, readily accepted the Nazi creed. The conquest of the Catholic Swabians took a longer time, but since the Austrian *Anschluss*, and still more since Munich, even among them all opposition to the Nazis has disappeared. During the mobilisation of March and April 1939, the German minority showed in many cases undisguised contempt for the Rumanians; and when in September 1939 the German armies advanced through Southern Poland towards Rumania, these Germans openly avowed themselves what Hitler means them to be: part of his " *Volk* ". Seeing what happened in Austria, Czechoslovakia, and Poland, a member of the German minority in Rumania hardly dares to keep out of the Nazi organisations, for fear of being treated, after a conquest by Germany, as a " *Volksverräter* ".

In Rumania, too, anti-Semitic legislation helps the Nazis to capture industry and trade; this was done in a more direct manner by " Aryanisation " in conquered Czechoslovakia and Poland. Nor can the Rumanian laws which restrict the business activities of foreigners stop the Nazis: the German minority step in as citizens of the country. And even more successful than in Hungary has proved in Rumania the Nazi currency trick:

> . . . Germany has paid preferential prices which have temporarily raised the standard of life of the Rumanian peasant farmer, but by pushing down the value of the lei against the mark, Germany herself pays less and less, while she pushes up prices inside Rumania. Even for the farmers the improvement is only temporary.

In Yugoslavia the conflict between Croats and Serbs, and even the widespread Serb opposition to the dictatorship and the Stoyadinovich administration, offered the Nazis rich opportunities for political intrigue; it is one of their regular methods " to play everywhere upon the difficulties between Government and governed, and by alarming rulers to impel them to take unpopular measures ". Every aspect of the Croat question was developed with customary zeal.

While official Germany had more and more

praised Stoyadinovich for his cold-shouldering of the Little Entente in favour of the Axis Powers, whisperers in Croatia had lavished sympathy upon the Croats in the oppression of their race by the alien Serb régime. The racial theories of a Croat writer named Sufflay were taken up since Sufflay had held that the Croats were not Slavs like the Serbs, but were the descendants of a settlement of Goths. This notion was to be found in the paper *Nezavismost* (Independence) brought out by a certain M. Buc who was obviously dependent upon German funds. It was characteristic of the whole situation that *Nezavismost* furiously attacked Dr. Macek for his moderation in championing the Croat national cause against the pro-German Stoyadinovich régime though M. Buc was supported by money from Germany.

While the Croats were thus intended for the part which the Slovaks had played in the disruption of Czechoslovakia, confidential instructions circulated by the Nazis among the German minority in Croatia described them as " half savage ".

> Mixed marriages are therefore condemned. Among other recommendations is one to avoid alcoholic drink but to sell it in as large quantities as possible to the Croats; on occasion the press of the Reich has supported an attitude of this kind.

The German minority, effectively organised by Nazi emissaries and leaders, at elections was made to support the Stoyadinovich régime against which the Croats were being incited. All districts of Yugoslavia comprising a German population were covered with branches of the *Kulturbund*, were given libraries stocked with Nazi literature, and were provided with German schools.

For all German propaganda unlimited funds were, as ever, available, and while the German Legation in Belgrade went through the usual process of *Gleichschaltung*, it was the German Consul-General, Herr Neuhausen, also at the head of the German Tourist Office, who appeared to be the most powerful link between Nazi Germany, Yugoslavia and its German minority. He represents various German business houses as well as the German State Railways and Lufthansa, while the *Dresdner Bank* works in connection with his Travel Bureaux, which are the centres of all German activity in Yugoslavia.

Germany's economic hold on Yugoslavia was even more complete than that on Hungary and Rumania; for economically Yugoslavia was more closely connected with Austria and Czechoslovakia, and since the conquest of these two countries Germany's investments in Yugoslavia outstrip those of any other country. The same methods as in Hungary and Rumania were practised to acquire a virtual monopoly of Yugoslavia's foreign trade. For several years past, Germany has bought Yugoslav agricultural products at prices at least 25 to 30 per cent above the world price level, and now compensates herself by manipulating the exchange. It is not easy to translate into exact figures this barter business, which is lauded by Nazi propaganda as something pure, simple, and noble, and contrasted with the money-economy and transactions of the Western Powers, the " démodé capitalism " of greedy foreign usurers, either Jews or men imbued with Jewish ideas.

THE GERMAN INTERNATIONAL

With Austria and Czechoslovakia engulfed in the German system, and Italy impoverished by the Abyssinian and Spanish wars, Yugoslavia was in danger of becoming more and more a German economic dependency.

Nazi relations with Poland cannot be treated at any length in this essay: and the transactions described by Miss Wiskemann, who finished writing her book before the outbreak of war, have by now been overlaid by mass outrages and crimes unprecedented in European records. When the history of the war is written, the services rendered by Germans domiciled in Poland as Nazi spies during the military campaign will deserve attention: they were widespread and effective, and remarkably well organised, and the Nazis succeeded in pressing into their service even many Germans settled in Poland for generations. Nor was the part of these " minority Germans " less discreditable after the Nazi régime had been established in Poland. In various parts of the country they have formed themselves into a " *Selbstschutz* " (self-defence) — what this is could easily be guessed, were guessing necessary. But an article in the *Völkischer Beobachter* openly boasts that men of this organisation " with their knowledge of the Polish language are able to trace the most secret places of refuge of Polish criminals, and have in every way proved the most efficient scouts ". Lastly, to be a " *Volksdeutscher* " in Poland under Nazi occupation is to be master of the lives and property of Poles and Jews; he is free to rob and kill, and only too many among the " minority " Germans in Poland seem to have taken advantage of the opportunities thus offered.

In view of the doctrine openly proclaimed by the Nazis that Germans, wherever born and of whatever State they are citizens, owe allegiance, first and foremost, to the German *Volk* and its Führer; in view of the use so effectively made of German minorities for the disruption or enslavement of the States in which they live; and lastly, in view of the behaviour of vast numbers, possibly of a majority, of the Germans inhabiting Poland — any State containing a German " Aryan " minority within its borders will have to consider in future whether it is safe to have them.

HITLER'S WAR

(" *The Nineteenth Century and After* ", *January* 1940)

HITLER, asked by a friend at what point he first gained the conviction that he would get the better of his German opponents, is said to have replied that he attained it after having been a week in prison: when he saw that they had neither executed nor poisoned him. This is what he would obviously have done to them. And he presumably gained the conviction that he would master Europe, when he saw himself left free to re-arm, and his most trivial explanations or excuses accepted by people who, however much they disapproved of his methods and actions, were not prepared to use violence against him. Every man has only one method, as he has only one face; he is born with both. Machiavelli knew it: he says that when a man's method suits the circumstances, we call it good luck, and when it does not, we call it bad luck. So far Hitler's method has served him well; with " somnambulant " but gangsterlike skill he has played on the consciences and fears of his opponents, and has exploited the mental and moral exhaustion of his contemporaries. He was dealing with men who would not assume the responsibility for preventive slaughter, even if the possible alternative were their own extinction; and with a tired, disillusioned world, which longed for rest.

There have been wars with restricted objectives and

wars for world hegemony; wars of purpose and wars of tension. They differ not only in size and duration, but in their emotional and spiritual background and in their modes of settlement. A war with a local objective, however basic that may be in its own sphere, is amenable to immediate settlement in territorial or constitutional terms; thus in 1866, once the Habsburgs had agreed to withdraw from Germany and Italy, the conflict was closed. But a war in which the issue is world hegemony *versus* a European balance of power has to be fought to the bitter end. The distinctive features of these contests have appeared with increasing clearness and compression in the wars of Louis XIV, of the French Revolution and Napoleon, and in the War of 1914–1918. These wars were preceded by periods of mental unrest and travail, and fought with a consciousness of their universal character and issue; changes of frontier or a return to the *status quo* offer no secure solution once the European system has been challenged. If 100,000 people within a certain area catch 100,000 seasonal but individual colds, this is still something very different from the same people succumbing to the great influenza, thus named by the Italians of the Renaissance because they knew that it returns in cycles " under the influence of the stars ". In fact, the great epidemics of influenza usually occur at intervals of twenty-seven years, and world wars at intervals of a century, that is to say, once in every three generations; and the sum-total of a number of wars with individual objectives, whatever it may be, differs radically from a world war.[1]

[1] An anonymous French treatise, *Débat des hérauts d'armes de France et d'Angleterre*, written between 1453 and 1461, distinguishes between " les

War-weariness tends to prevent a more frequent recurrence of the great contests for predominance. Two generations of Frenchmen chafed and fretted under the Treaty of Vienna, talked about *la maladie de 1815* and about *le poignant souvenir de Waterloo*, boasted of its being the fate of France to keep her neighbours " in a state of perpetual apprehension ", and called it her glory and danger. Still, at heart they themselves desired peace, and their protestations and threats *n'étaient qu'un tapage superficiel et restreint*. Guizot thus wrote about the thirties of the last century:

> Never had so many causes for war occurred in so few years. . . . In the past, it would have broken out, I know not how many times, and lasted, I know not how long; in our days there was hardly a move in that direction, and whenever it occurred, it was partial and short-lived; everywhere there was haste to stop it. . . . Peace withstood and survived all dangers.

Some twenty years later the first plebiscitarian dictator, Napoleon III, in a vague and confused manner sought a sham reversal of the Treaty of Vienna in a war carried on jointly with Great Britain. Problems of power politics loomed in the background, but as

grandes et nobles guerres, les guerres de magnificence " and " les guerres de frontières . . . guerres communes ", which hardly deserve attention. Subsequent experience has led Frenchmen to form a different estimate of the two kinds of war: Henri IV, Richelieu, and Mazarin, who fought for better frontiers, are now looked upon as the master builders of France, while Louis XIV and Napoleon, who pursued grandiose dreams of dominion, are seen to have dissipated her assets and undermined her position. An analogous estimate will probably be made some day of Frederick II and Bismarck on the one hand, and William II and Hitler on the other.

mankind was not ripe for one of the major conflicts, the Crimean War followed an uncertain, halting course, and, in the absence of sufficient local purpose, has gone down to history as the most senseless of all wars.

Is the present war a World War? Will it last, will it grow? Never have the nations involved in a conflict of such magnitude entered it with so little zest and with so few hopes or dreams of a better future; in fact, with such reluctance. There have been no scenes of naive enthusiasm, no outbursts of national hatred: the usual antecedents of war, or circumstances attendant on its outbreak, were lacking. In Germany there was a universal wishful disbelief that the Western Powers would go to war, or that, having done so, they would persist in carrying it through; in this country and in France there was a painful consciousness that we had no choice in the matter, and that at any price an end must be made to the intolerable alarms and developments of the last few years.

Terror, physical terror, is to Hitler an instrument of policy; for individuals he has torture, and for nations threats of destruction by mysterious new weapons. But a bully is not necessarily a fighter, any more than a blackmailer is a publicist; both prefer to " negotiate ". Hitler, therefore, while re-arming on a scale hitherto unknown in peace-time, never ceased protesting, perhaps not altogether insincerely, his readiness to renounce war: at a price. And like the typical blackmailer he never named his total price (to which, indeed, there is no limit), but while his exactions were growing, each time solemnly declared that this particular demand was absolutely the last which he would ever make.

Mankind was intellectually and emotionally unprepared to re-enter upon a major conflict; and among the free nations the passionate loathing of war found its material expression in the (otherwise inexplicable and inexcusable) technical unpreparedness of the Western democracies. Hitler alone had the supreme tactical advantage of being able to disregard the war-weariness and fears of his own people: that a-moral paranoiac is in control of a mechanised nation, as dirigible, insensitive, and merciless as a machine. He has shown intuitive cleverness in exploiting the situation. He has tried to reverse the verdict and destroy the results of a World War by breaking up the issue into a series of restricted local claims. As he proceeded, his action was quickening and gathering momentum; his ways and the spirit in which he was working were obvious, and yet he was allowed to proceed: a hypnotic paralysis seemed to hold down his intended victims. But at times he himself would avow both his method and his ultimate purpose: to tear up the Treaty of Versailles, page by page.

That treaty was for Hitler the blackmailer's lucky find — not the real treaty, but the legends built up around it. He did not start them (it is amazing how little inventive capacity he has shown in an almost unique career), but he has put them to the fullest and foulest use.

First there was the story about the " stab in the back," comforting to German pride: the German armies had not been defeated in the field, but sabotaged by revolution at home. In reality never has better testimony been borne to Sorel's dictum that revolution does not destroy a government but breaks out on its collapse, than by Germany in November 1918. Mildly critical henchmen of the previous régime, with a heavy heart, stepped into the place vacated by it; and, pressed by the High Command, concluded a peace with which they, the " Weimar scoundrels ", were to be taxed ever after.

Secondly, there was the story about the blandishments and the deceit of the Allies: Germany had cheerfully called out for peace, because it had suddenly struck her how very nice a reconciliation would be, and then the outrageous Versailles Treaty was imposed on her. This treaty was, in fact, eminently fair and reasonable with regard to frontiers, the most important, because the most permanent, feature of treaties. But its hysterical traducers, British or German, if silenced on this point, burble about war-guilt, *Diktat*, reparations, and the disarming of Germany. The war-guilt clause was unnecessary and therefore silly, but not untrue; negotiations produced a change in the draft treaty which was important and was unfair to the Poles; and reparations were eventually evaded and defeated by the Germans. In one matter the treaty did err: in depriving the German people of its army. This set a high premium on Hitler's jack-boots and *ersatz* uniforms.[1]

After Hitler had established new records in calumny, dictation, and barefaced stealing of property, and the Germans themselves had paid to him more than had ever been demanded of them in reparations, a third

[1] Disarmament can only be effective if accompanied by a measure of permanent occupation.

legend arose, not complimentary, but highly advantageous to him. People in this country who abhorred his actions volunteered to shoulder his guilt: we and our misdeeds were to blame for his rise. This was an exoneration of Germany; to Hitler it was a basis for expiatory demands.

Had there ever been a chance of a different Germany arising after 1918? The so-called " revolution " of that year had wrought no basic change, and the " European " pacifism of the Weimar parties was inspired by an uneasy opportunism, not by any new conceptions or ideas. Before the collapse, Stresemann had applauded Brest-Litovsk; Erzberger had been an agent of Imperial intrigue; Scheidemann would have been satisfied with the " liberalism " of a Kühlmann. Nor did these men stand for a new outlook or creed in home affairs; they timidly gazed at those whom they had replaced (not displaced), and when attacked from the Right, lacked the courage to resist. There was popular unrest and inarticulate passions. They never found a vent under the Weimar Republic: Hitler supplied it.

German aristocratic Conservatism perished in the *débâcle* of 1918; German middle-class self-sufficiency in the *déroute* of inflation; while the organised working classes intent on rational progress were a creation, or fiction, of the Radical intelligentsia. Conservatives, Liberals, and Socialists did not understand how close they were to each other: children of the same period and civilisation, though differing in age, they quarrelled in the same language. And they, all alike, committed the same mistake with regard to Hitler: they thought that he could be fitted into their world, taught to speak their language and transact business in their own way. The Conservatives expected Nazism to do their work, to divert popular passions into anti-Semitic channels, and then remain a regulated river within the banks assigned to it. The Socialists hoped that Hitler would undergo the sobering influence of office — they thought that he, too, merely talked violence. The Nazis made no original contribution to political or economic thought, but there was a new reality in them: the coarse or insane sadism of the mentally, morally, and materially dispossessed, which raised violence to the level of a principle, and sanctified it by group-glorification. Even after the miscalculations of the German political parties had become manifest, they still found their exact counterpart abroad: the enemies of Communism in other countries believed that Hitler would prove a helpful exponent of their creed, while foreign Governments hoped that the sobering influence of office would force and fit him into their ways — misconceptions which were to play once more into Hitler's hands.

No peace treaty, however good, could by its results have satisfied the world. In the grey aftermath of war sensitive consciences cried out for a millennium which alone could have justified *ex post* the slaughter of millions. Regret and disappointment were bound to follow. And as Hitler blustered and threatened, pangs of conscience were felt about the Treaty of Versailles, while worse treaties remained forgotten. This was not mere hypocrisy or fear — behind it was the passionate desire of a war-weary world to believe that it was still in its power to preserve peace. There was hope and comfort in guilt: better ways were to placate German wrath. But Hitler was soon to prove, beyond all doubt, that this was not a question of repairing minor mistakes, real or alleged. The atrocious and wholly senseless anti-Jewish pogrom of November 1938, following immediately on Munich, freed many hesitant consciences of their imaginary guilt; the "rape of Czechoslovakia" in March 1939 completed their release. The problem of European and, ultimately, of world hegemony was now starkly reopened in the sign of a savage rule.

Hitler had cleverly exploited the weariness, the fears, the scruples, and the regrets of minds and characters much finer and more complex than his own, but he never understood their working, nor appreciated their motives. The blackmailer did not expect to be brought into court, nor the bully to have to fight. And yet this war is his war, and nobody else's. He has forced it upon people who, passionately averse to war, had borne with him far too long, even against their own better judgment.

1812 AND 1941

("The Times," January 13, 1942)

THERE are situations inherent in the structure of Europe, and enduring tendencies in the character of nations. It would be as idle to say that " history does not repeat itself " as to base repetitive expectations on dates, places, and casual circumstances. Moreover, the war of 1812 supplies a unique precedent and pattern for that of 1941; its campaign has been the subject of the closest study by both the German and Russian General Staffs; and it lives in the consciousness of both nations.

Revolutionary and Napoleonic France had a far greater population than any other Continental Power (barring Russia); national cohesion and the *élan* of a revolutionary idea; a better military organisation and superior leadership; and till 1813 the advantage of never having to fight a united Europe. The English Channel and the expanse of Russia ultimately defeated Napoleon. Nazi Germany similarly had the initial advantages of numbers, *élan*, military organisation, and generalship; of an even more central position; and of never having to deal with a united Europe. The German campaigns were as carefully planned and prepared as those of Napoleon: team-work replaced genius (Hitler's share, whatever it may be, does not extend to technical direction); there was timing and speed —

like Napoleon, the Germans alone seemed to understand their value. By June 1941 Germany dominated the Continent as Napoleon had in 1810: Great Britain was equally isolated in Europe. Napoleon and Hitler both had their agreements with Russia, and their suspicions of her. Baulked by the Channel, both saw their chance of coming to grips with England across Turkey; but could Russia, on their flank, have remained indifferent to either of them crossing the Straits?

The Polish problem, however much Napoleon tried to evade it, stood between him and Russia; ideological differences, however much Hitler tried to cover them up, stood between him and Stalin. Alexander and Stalin both saw that, sooner or later, they would be forced to fight Europe's dictator. But here the analogy ends: in 1811 Napoleon obtained knowledge of Alexander's having thought of attacking him; no such accusation could honestly be raised against Russia in 1941. On the other hand the need of coming to grips with England was more pressing in 1941 than in 1812. Hitler obviously valued Russia's strength (and Stalin's statesmanship) sufficiently high not to risk sending the bulk of his forces across the Straits before having finished with her; and sufficiently low to imagine that this was a summer's work. Turkey could not have withstood his full strength longer than had Poland, France, or Yugoslavia; and by reaching the vicinity of Baku and Batum he would have obtained a stranglehold on Russia. But was Russia sufficiently prepared to counter him in time? Obviously the Germans would take no risks: they are hypersensitive where a possible invasion of their own country is concerned.

1812 AND 1941

Material about the campaign of 1812 abounds, and a most comprehensive and masterly digest of it is given in a work, published in 1937, by General Marian Kukiel,[1] at present G.O.C. the Polish troops in Scotland. About the campaign now in progress information is necessarily scanty and uncertain. But the question is ever present in people's minds: How do the two compare? There have been revolutionary changes in transport and armament. None the less, so far the Channel has played its historic part: will the expanse and climate of Russia play its part a second time?

There was boastful challenge to history and fate in Hitler choosing June 22 for his attack on Russia — the day on which Napoleon had opened his. In 1812 delay was due to political hesitations and to supply problems: Napoleon's army comprised 600,000 men and (for speed and mobility) over 150,000 horses; he needed fresh crops and green fodder. Yugoslavia and Crete may have delayed Hitler's start: some think that it was only the Russian treaty with Yugoslavia of April 5 which clinched his resolve to attack Russia. At the outset Napoleon had an army twice as big as the Russian; lengthening lines of communication and losses caused by the rapid advance established approximate equality on the Moskva; much heavier Russian casualties at Borodino unsettled it once more. German numbers were probably inferior, though not at the outset when they took the Russians by surprise. Napoleon and the Germans had the advantage of better organisation and equipment, superior strategy, and of the consciousness of never yet having suffered defeat.

[1] *Wojna 1812 roku.* 2 vols. Cracow, 1937.

1812 AND 1941

Only one-third of Napoleon's army was French, one-third German, one-seventh Polish, and the rest Italian, Spanish, Dutch, etc. In Hitler's armies allies or janissaries form a much smaller proportion. The Russian armies were, and are, more homogeneous than either. Their approach to both wars is the same.

> The Russian armies [writes General Kukiel] entered the war of 1812 conscious of having to deal with an opponent superior numerically, tactically, and intellectually. . . . Lauriston reported from St. Petersburg, and Narbonne from Vilna, the absence of "all fanfaronade". But echoes of what the Russians were saying reached the Napoleonic armies: "We shall fight, and they must kill us in order to defeat us." It should be stated that this was no empty boast.

Similarly their fighting qualities have remained the same: great tenacity, courage, and endurance; supreme skill in guerrilla fighting; fanaticism, and "psychic resistance to defeat". At Borodino the Russians lost half their effectives; here is General Kukiel's account, written in 1937:

> The Russian army retreated . . . without demoralisation or decomposition. "Its body was stricken, not its spirit", wrote Saint-Cyr. Reduced numerically, it did not cease to be an effective instrument of war. The incredible moral staying power and stoicism of the Russian army of 1812 introduced an unknown factor into all calculations based on material forces. . . . In the night after the battle Napoleon entertained the hope — and many shared it — that the end had

been reached through the annihilation of the Russian forces. He was wrong.

Napoleon had a sufficient initial superiority of numbers to attack on a wide front, but he concentrated on the Vilna–Smolensk–Moscow line practically all his army, neglecting its flanks and adding to the difficulties of provisioning it; he counted on a decisive blow against Moscow producing moral and political collapse. The Germans, too, although they advanced along the entire front, made their main initial effort against Moscow, obviously on the same political grounds; when stopped east of Smolensk, they developed the essentially " material " attack in the south. Napoleon counted on (but failed in the long run to promote) a rising of the Polish gentry in Lithuania and White Russia, which remained ineffective; thought of raising a peasant movement in Central Russia; and dreamt of (non-existent) *boyar* discontent in Moscow. But it was only in the west, where the landowners were Polish, that Napoleon could have raised a Russian peasant revolt, and there he did not want it (its mere shadow had a damping effect on the Poles). In Central Russia, beyond the old Polish frontier of 1772, he met with relentless, universal hostility: with a most determined Russian national movement. The Germans received help from some of the Baltic peoples (and failed to requite it); counted on hostility against the Soviets in the Ukraine, and failed to find it; and never expected the degree of national unity and enthusiasm with which they have to contend: this alone renders possible a " scorched earth " policy and guerrilla warfare.

Napoleon and Hitler both aimed at a short war and

battles of annihilation. Alexander said, " On my side are space and time ". Gneisenau advised him to prolong the war, lay waste the country, play for a winter campaign: the French soldier would not be able to endure it. Rostopchin wrote to him that, should circumstances force him to retreat, he would " always be powerful in Moscow, menacing at Kazan, and invincible at Tobolsk ". Thus what happened had been foreseen: although repeatedly both Tsar and generals tried to deviate from the programme, and resist. In 1941 again a retreat was foreseen: hence the transfer of war industries beyond the Volga during the preceding years. None the less, the war production of the Leningrad and Moscow regions, and of the south, remained too important lightly to admit of a retreat.

Geographical difficulties were reduced by modern transport and armament; but the Russian resistance was very much greater in 1941 than in 1812. Napoleon reached Smolensk on August 16-18; the Germans at the end of July. But he reached Mozhaisk on September 9; they at the end of October. Winter in 1941 set in about a month later than in 1812: it is amazing that it should have found the Germans almost as poorly clothed as Napoleon's army. But Napoleon and Hitler both expected to conclude the campaign, or to arrest it, before the winter. Napoleon's generals urged him to stop at Vitebsk or Smolensk; the same is said about Hitler and his generals. The lure of Moscow proved too strong for both.

Now the Germans are retreating. It is as yet a very different retreat from that of 1812. Even while Napoleon's army was advancing, discipline was far from good; without its collapse the disaster could not have assumed such appalling dimensions. Still, the problems facing the German command are grave: it seems doubtful whether a front of 2000 miles can be stabilised in the Russian winter, while a mechanised army can hardly retreat through a snow-bound country without abandoning most of its equipment. And the men? When in 1830 there was talk of French intervention in Russia, Pushkin invited them to come:

> Is there not room for the graves of all of you in Russia, Among graves not strange to you?

The graves of 1812 harbour Germans no less than Frenchmen.

SYMMETRY AND REPETITION

("*Manchester Guardian*", *January* 1, 1941)

THE effort which people put up to avoid thinking might almost enable them to think and to have some new ideas. But having ideas produces anxiety and *malaise* and runs counter to the deepest instincts of human nature, which loves symmetry, repetition, and routine. Mine certainly does, and to such a degree that I get sick of them, and then notice that proclivity in others and criticise it.

When an East European peasant sits to a photographer, he places his hands symmetrically on his knees, like the statues of the Pharaohs: obviously a primeval instinct. Italian peasants and *petit bourgeois* cannot stand asymmetry in the distribution of windows, and paint them on the wall if it is impossible to have real ones in their place. German faces are marvellously symmetrical — look, for instance, at that of Hindenburg. No other European nation ever attains that square, stolid facial symmetry. The love which the Germans have for symmetry, repetition, and routine helps to make them great organisers.

One would expect people to remember the past and to imagine the future. But in fact, when discoursing or writing about history, they imagine it in terms of their own experience, and when trying to gauge the future they cite supposed analogies from the past: till, by a double process of repetition, they imagine the past and remember the future.

There are fetishes of dates, places, and methods. One of the reasons of the Austrian disaster in Serbia, in August 1914, was that the Austrian commander made haste to have a victory for the Emperor Francis Joseph's birthday, which fell on the 18th of that month. The date and region of Sedan were not without influence on the German operations which preceded the first Battle of the Marne; nor again was the name in 1940. On the other hand, the memory of defeats turned into victories cheered the British public in May 1940, especially as the retreating armies approached the Marne. When the possibility of successful resistance vanished in France one weighty reason against her continuing it from the colonies was that the French had never done so before. The editor of *La France Libre* writes in a brilliant article on " La Capitulation ": " L'idée de défendre la France de l'extérieur restait abstraite, parce qu'aucun souvenir, aucune tradition ne l'animait ". Our own memories of the last war are of the battles of Ypres, the Somme, Vimy Ridge, and Passchendaele, and we therefore do not relish the idea of fighting in Flanders and France, but should cheerfully take to action in Spain, for then we should have a Peninsular War of blessed memory.

Among the German troops now in Poland the best-behaved are those who had been there with the German army of occupation in the last war, partly because these are older men who have not been in the Hitler Youth, but partly because they remember how, after having conquered country after country, Germany collapsed.

"Last time," said such a soldier to a Pole a year ago, "I was disarmed by a washerwoman. I wonder who will disarm me this time?" The memories of 1918 weigh on the Germans. On the other hand, the Italians are fortified in their misfortunes by remembering that they never won a battle (unless both sides were Italian), but invariably managed to profit by somebody else's victory (the fame of Garibaldi as a soldier rests on his having fought only Italians). "When the Cardinal of Rouen said to me that the Italians had no aptitude for war," wrote Machiavelli four centuries ago, "I answered him that the French had no aptitude for politics." In another passage, while giving copious excuses, Machiavelli admits that "in all the many wars of the last twenty years, whenever an army was wholly Italian it failed to stand the test".

A book could be written on the plagiarism of revolutions. The imaginative and emotional element is strong in them, and while objective observation and thought draws on the infinite variety of nature, human imagination and feelings are restricted and stereotyped. Most novelists or dramatists have only one or two plots, which they adorn with artificial variations, and Napoleon fought all his battles on two variations of one single plan, confessing at St. Helena that in his last battle he did not know more than in his first. Revolutions have their tradition, ritual, and magic tricks; moreover, it is easy to acquire the habit of revolutions: revolution breeds revolution. To quote Machiavelli once more: "Perchè sempre una mutazione lascia lo addentellato per la edificazione dell' altra" ("For one change always leaves an indent for the next ").

SYMMETRY AND REPETITION

Continuity is a compromise between novelty and repetition. "The English angel of progress moves from precedent to precedent", and that is why we are invariably well prepared to fight the previous war. In 1914 we had the equipment and training which would have served us well in the Boer War, and in 1939 we had all that was needed in 1914. The French held in 1914 ideas about offensive action inappropriate to trench warfare, and in 1939 ideas based on trench warfare irrelevant to a war of movement. The position of the Poles was even worse. They had, for a century, been without State and army, and when they had left off, the cavalry of Jan Sobieski and of the Napoleonic Legions had still a *raison d'être*; so they prepared an excellent and numerous cavalry for a war of tanks and aeroplanes. I asked a Polish officer why they had done so. He replied that they had prepared for war with Russia rather than with Germany. "But Russia, too, has a mechanised army," I remarked. He answered that this was so.

It is a mistake to suppose that people think: they wobble with the brain, and sometimes the brain does not wobble.

THE MISSING GENERATION

("*The Spectator, March* 21, 1941)

In *The Spectator* of April 12, 1940, Mr. Harold Nicolson, when discussing the argument which attributes the "apparent dearth of rising statesmen" to "a whole generation" having been destroyed in the last war, pointed out that, for instance, "many of those who were at Oxford during that most legendary period from 1905 to 1914 survived the war", including some who at the time were regarded as even abler than those who died — "yet only a small minority of those have risen to positions of power". "Janus" in *The Spectator* of March 7, 1941, shows that percentually the losses of the last war do not justify the talk about a "missing generation". To this might be added that, had the losses been even greater, a certain measure of substitution could have been expected: as with trees, when an essential branch is cut off, another which normally would not have played the part tends to replace it. Seldom has there been such destruction of actual and potential leaders, political, military, and intellectual, as in the French Revolution, but was there a shortage during the years 1795–1815? On the contrary: the void offered exceptional chances to new men, who took them. If it were merely a question of the "missing generation", why have not younger men replaced it in recent years? Hardly anyone who is 40 has fought in the last war, having been under 18 at the Armistice. By now the post-war generation has had time to come to the fore. Mr. Gladstone was 40 in 1849, Lord Balfour in 1888, Lord Randolph Churchill in 1889, Lord Birkenhead in 1912, Mr. Winston Churchill in 1914. They had to compete with an older generation not thinned out by war: still, each of them had at that age reached the front rank of politics.

In France politicians, on the whole, make their mark at a comparatively young age, and yet the post-war generation has produced nobody. Even more striking is the lowering of the level in her art and literature, in which supreme quality is usually discernible before 40. The post-war period has produced no new names which could compare with Zola, Anatole France, Cézanne, Renoir, Gauguin, or Rodin in an older generation, or with Gide, Proust, Romains, Péguy, Matisse, Derain, or Maillol among the younger men. Still more surprising is the change in Poland (of which the largest part, late Russian Poland, lost comparatively few men in the last war, as it soon came under enemy occupation and therefore had few classes conscripted for the army). With national independence regained, magnificent developments might have been expected: but while during the twenty years preceding 1914, Polish literature reached a level surpassed only once, by the peaks of the Romantic period 1820–1850, and never equalled in the sum-total of achievement, during the twenty years 1919–1939 it produced next to nothing. In Polish politics nearly everyone now in the forefront was known in 1919, or even in 1914.

It is not a generation which seems to have perished

in the last war, but an atmosphere, an inspiration, *un élan vital* — and their loss has deadened the living. Statesmen, artists, and writers work against a social background, on values and ideas produced in the common national existence. Where the deeper fellowship breaks up, where collective aims fade, where men no longer cherish common hopes but in disappointment turn to their own individual concerns and seek comfort in good living, little scope and incentive is left for statesmanship, and contests and controversies, which are part of political life, assume a personal, pernicious, poisonous character. Were there no bitter contests in France before 1914, were there no hostilities between her statesmen or generals during the war? Yet none assumed the deadly character of those of 1939–1940 — "*il y avait la France*". Why wonder that in this country there has been little rise, and even less selection, from the ranks of the younger generations, when the artificers of victory, still in full vigour, were discarded and replaced by men of their own age, but untried, inexperienced, and undistinguished? If in 1922 the most competent political observers had been asked who would govern Great Britain during the next eighteen years, not one would have named Mr. MacDonald, Lord Baldwin, and Mr. Neville Chamberlain.

There was a feeling of fatigue. The strain, physical, mental, and emotional, had been too great. The country was weary and worried. Eagles and lions would have been out of place, almost laughable: no one wanted to soar or to roar. There was no call for experiment and adventure, for bold, imaginative leadership, for greatness. There was disappointment. People did not want to be reminded of the war, not so much because of its sufferings and sacrifices, as because of its unfulfilled and utterly unattainable expectations, which, none the less, had helped us to go through with it. The country muddled along. If there were survivors of the war generation, or post-war young men, fit to speak a different language, the stage was not set for them, their appeal would have sounded false and hollow, the words would have died on their lips, they would have relapsed into the void. Generations were not missing; but there was nothing for them to do or to say. Looking back at those years one wonders at their stale, sterile spirit and at their leaders.

The disenchantment of victory is far more paralysing than the bitterness of defeat. The Western democracies — America, Great Britain, and France — seemed to have the world in their power; except that it is not in the power of men to remake worlds. Had we had the inspiration, humility, and sanity of true Conservatism, had we had a firm, feasible purpose and the determination to carry it through, we might at least have preserved the obvious fruits of war and victory. Far more was desired, infinitely less was achieved. In this war we are fully conscious of fighting for our very life as a civilised nation: the war has to be fought through to the bitter end — an end much more complete and decisive than 1918 — even if nothing more can be achieved by victory than bare survival. In the last war we had still visions of a world better than that which we had known — of some glorious expiation for all the sufferings and deaths; and in a naive way we expected victory by itself to achieve our aims. The sacrifices made by France were even greater, the disappointment even more poignant. More than anything, this explains the spiritual listlessness of post-war France, her purely defensive attitude, and her downfall.

In Germany the bitterness of defeat planted the seeds of a purpose. An *élan* of rage was born of an exasperated " will to power ", of a fury of revenge in a nation singularly brutal and ruthless, and of the wrong idea, fostered by the restraint and mildness of the democratic Powers, that Germany had never been squarely beaten. On this negative basis the Nazis unified Germany and produced a statesmanship of their own. Their purpose may be vile, their methods atrocious; but their technique was certainly superior to that of the statesmen of the European democracies who faced them before, and at the outbreak of, the war. The losses of the war generation in Germany were percentually even greater than in this country; still, when there was an idea — no matter what its moral value or character — the Germans found within that so-called " missing generation " the men to carry it through. We have rediscovered real leaders only when the supreme danger to our existence and the instinct of self-preservation created a new national sense and unity. They will not be less needed after the victory is won.

GERMANY

I. NATIONAL CHARACTER

("The Spectator", February 28, 1941)

WHENEVER the German national character is discussed, someone will invariably remark that he has known such decent, kindly Germans, and will protest against " generalisations "; without perceiving that it is he who is advancing an unwarrantable generalisation in arguing about the character of a nation from that of individuals, often of individuals met outside their own national surroundings. Even with regard to inanimate matter it is unsafe to argue from particles to aggregates: the atom is the same in graphite and in diamonds; and it is not possible from the way in which a lump of coal burns to infer the behaviour of an entire bed of the same coal. Aggregates have their own individuality and laws.

A social agglomeration can be a crowd or an organised unit, individuals in mass juxtaposition or in crystallised form. The psychological peculiarities even of the crowd vary as between different nations. But still greater and more significant are the differences between the forms of communal life which nations have developed, and the variations in the degree of freedom or of moral sense which these forms present, preserve, or attain. A nation can crystallise above or below the average moral level of the individuals who compose it.

GERMANY

Most types of social groups can be found, in one form or another, in all nations, but attaining various degrees of development and importance; and some nations develop one or two forms into dominant patterns which express the national character and their communal life. Thus the pattern forms of England are Parliament and the team, of Germany the State and the army, or perhaps rather the army and the State. Characteristic of the English social groups is the degree of freedom which they leave to the individual and the basic equality of their members, the voluntary submission to the rules of " the game " and the curious mixture of elasticity and rigidity in these rules; most of all, the moral standards which these groups enforce or to which they aspire. Characteristic of the German social groups is the utter, conscious, subordination of the individual, the iron discipline which they enforce, the high degree of organisation and efficiency which they attain, and their resultant inhumanity. The State is an aim in itself, while that of the army is essentially a-moral — to smash the enemy. Whatever characteristics in the individual members of the two nations have gone to form these patterns, and whatever share circumstances had in their development, once crystallised these patterns powerfully react on the individual and mould him in turn. Removed from this setting the individual may develop, or at least seem to develop, in a different manner: still, it is the pattern which expresses his national character.

The English national pattern raises individuals above their own average moral level, the German suppresses their human sides. Religious Puritanism, with its more modern offshoots, was perhaps the most potent factor in the moulding of the English national character: the English gentleman is the spiritual heir of the Puritans rather than of the Cavaliers. But the Puritans, in spite of, or perhaps because of, their intense basic individualism, insisted on men living in communities. To this day there is a visible difference between the countryside of, say, New York State and Connecticut — on the one side scattered farms, on the other clustered townships. For the Puritans did not allow men to live in solitude, believing that the control and corrective of the group was necessary to maintain the highest moral standards in the individual. The tale about the Englishman who dining alone in the desert puts on his dinner-jacket, is of a man who, far away from his group, tries to preserve its code, in matters great and small.

With the Germans savagery is deliberately inculcated; they are the only European nation which glories in the barbaric period of its history, and they bear all the marks of it. They call it being "hard" — Hitler boasts of being "the hardest German that ever lived" — and they look upon brutality as the highest form of strength. Madame de Staël, writing about 1810, remarked that there seems to be no connexion between the German's thoughts and his nature; and in our own time some perfect brutes among the Germans have written wonderfully delicate lyrics. Even in the war of 1870, the behaviour of the German officers was notoriously worse than that of the common soldiers. In the Great War, "frightfulness" was prescribed by the German army regulations. The worst Nazi atrocities, both at home and abroad, have been systematically planned and organised from above. Still, hundreds of thousands of men have participated in them, and tens of millions have watched them with approval, or at least with connivance. The " decent, kindly Germans " were always singularly ineffective, in 1848 as in 1900 or under the Weimar Republic — many of them were Jews, and the others were looked upon as " *verjudet* " (" Judaised "). They have failed to impress their pattern on the nation, and to " generalise " their type or creed; it is therefore in turn inadmissible to base generalisations on them.

There are people who treat all evil as extraneous and adventitious: to them a sick person is a healthy person plus a disease, not a body in a condition which, whether temporary or permanent, is its own. A similar " demonology " treats the present Germany as a country of normal, decent people bewitched by Hitler; whereas in reality Hitler's unparalleled rise is due to the fact that he has given expression to some of the deepest instincts of the Germans. His creed follows the pattern of German national crystallisation. " He has spoken from their soul." He is probably one of the most representative Germans that ever lived — this is an unpleasant, indeed, painful fact, but which has to be faced. Hitler has conquered German youth. And how deep Nazism is rooted in the German nature can be gauged by the way in which Germans, especially of the younger generation, have, in remote continents, responded to its call — in the United States, Brazil, South Africa, etc.; still more, of course, in Central and South-Eastern Europe. Is there one German community abroad in which the anti-Nazis, though secure, independent, or even favoured by the nation in whose midst they live, have established a real ascendancy over the Nazis? where the " decent, kindly German ", that charming figure of the romantic legend, is anything more than a lost lamb?

The only pattern of crystallisation which the German nation has so far successfully produced is, at the best, one of a-moral force, which in action turns into the most savage instrument of destruction. And the problem which Europe, indeed the world, has had to face for some time past, without proving specially clever in handling it, is how to prevent the Germans from crystallising, that is, from achieving their characteristic social formations, the Leviathan State and the Prussian Army.

II. NAMES AND REALITIES

(" *Time and Tide* ", May 17, 1941)

Open any paper and you will find, " Hitler sees ", " Hitler thinks ", " Hitler wants ", " Hitler has struck ", " Hitler, checked at this point, will press in another direction . . ." If not omniscient or omnipotent, he certainly is made to appear ubiquitous. A hundred times a day, when it would be more correct to speak of Germany, the German Supreme Command, the German Foreign Office, etc., writers find it easier and more convenient to say for short: " Hitler ". He may be a more effective, and in that sense a greater, man than most of us thought him a few years ago; some of the most important and, from the German point of view, most profitable, decisions (such as the remilitarisation of the Rhineland and the invasion of Austria) are said to have been taken by him against determined opposition from his expert advisers. None the less, this constant use of his name is vastly exaggerated, and tends to build up a legend round him: it is, in certain ways, an unconscious and unintentional English equivalent of " Heil Hitler ", not, of course, of a morally laudatory, but of a magnifying, repetitive character. On our side, Mr. Churchill has probably a greater share in deciding war policy than Hitler in Germany; he works more steadily and much harder, has an infinitely greater knowledge and experience; still, writers do not operate with his name as they do with that of Hitler. The achievements and the guilt of Germany are not to be ascribed to one individual, nor even to a Party; they are the work of the German nation.

This raises another, even more important, problem of names; people operate with the description of " Nazi " as if it denoted a species of Germans extraneous to the nation, or at least as rare and isolated as the quislings are in Norway or Holland. But what is it which justifies us in dissociating any substantial part of the German nation from the " Nazis "? Undoubtedly, after Germany has been defeated, many Germans will deprecate and deplore a policy and actions which miscarried (some forty years ago a German writer explained: " *Laster ist ein mythologischer Ausdruck für schlechte Geschäfte* " — " Vice is a mythological description for unprofitable transactions "); but the Germans now take a full share in these transactions and endorse, extol, and turn them to their own personal profit. Are any cases known of sabotage committed by anti-Nazi Germans since the outbreak of war? Tens of thousands, if not hundreds of thousands, of Germans are taking part in the unspeakable oppression and spoliation of conquered, or of merely occupied, countries — are any cases known of Germans having crossed a neutral frontier (of which there were many in the past, and some exist even now), because they would no longer participate in such villainies? There are thousands of German airmen flying through the free air, sent to destroy open towns and to machine-gun civilians: has any German ever flown across to the Allies in protest, refusing to go on with the task assigned to him by commanders from whom he differed in spirit and outlook? There are numerous Germans employed abroad, by no means all of them original Nazis — has one of them resigned in protest against some new German outrage? Herr von Neurath is a typical representative of the pre-Nazi German civil service, and he enjoyed a high reputation in this country — what was his record in the Czech *Protektorat* over which he presided? Ten righteous men were the quota set for Sodom and Gomorrah, presumably from among a few thousand inhabitants: in proportion, probably at least 100,000 should be demanded from the German nation, and that of racially pure, uncontaminated Germans — *rassenreine Volksgenossen*. Where are they?

Without the active, wholehearted, indeed enthusiastic, support of the great body of the German nation, the original Nazis could never have achieved what, on the technical side, must now be placed to the credit of

Germany, and on the moral, be counted to her shame. The original Nazis and their associates had neither the ability nor the knowledge to build up and equip armies, and to devise and direct the colossal enterprise of modern war as it has been developed by the Germans. Not even as administrators are they anything but a liability and a clog; the Nazi *Gauleiters* are notoriously crude and corrupt. The patient, effective work of planning and carrying through destruction comes from Germans educated under a different system, but now harnessed body and soul to the Nazi régime. What Hitler and his gang have contributed is bold and uninhibited, fanatically blind, leadership; they could not have succeeded had they not moved along lines marked out by German history and by the German national *Geist* (genius). It is nonsense to suggest that the gigantic effort of this war could be wrung from an unwilling nation by terrorist means. Hitler understood the German people, which has found its full self-expression under his leadership. In this sense it is right to identify Hitler, the Nazis, and the German nation. But it is wrong, by the now current use of names, to credit Hitler with all the achievements, or to debit Hitler and the Nazis with all the guilt, while leaving out Germany and the Germans.

A year ago, the late Rudolf Olden, a German Liberal and an anti-Nazi, wrote a book to show that a different Germany could have arisen.[1] It is sincere and yet unconvincing, and ends with a passage fit to raise serious doubts and apprehensions in the mind of the reader:

[1] *Is Germany a Hopeless Case?*

If, instead of the excitable agitator, some better prince of average quality had been made Kaiser, if, instead of six years, twenty or thirty years had been given to the business, if some part at any rate of the public opinion of other countries had not been exasperated, if more reputable forms had been observed all through, then indeed the German danger might really one day have become tremendously formidable.

It is not for me to plead for Herr Hitler. But it may well be that the world has reason to be grateful to him. His folly, the inevitable impatience of the usurper, has perhaps saved the world from worse things. Those who set him up and made him supreme war-lord did a bad day's work, and some day they may rue it.

In other words, behind the wild Nazi façade, there is indeed "another Germany", less crude, less hysterical, but even more dangerous. It accepted the "co-operation" of the Nazis and aided their rise in order to appeal to the masses, whom the land-owning *Junkers*, the big industrialists, and the old German bureaucracy could not have won over in terms of their own *Weltanschauung*. But in Germany the mild, intellectual Liberals (supported largely by the Jews, who now have been "liquidated" by the Nazis for good and all) had even less influence and popularity than the old Conservatives, who had at least a tradition behind them; and whatever the sins of the Allied Powers, even from Herr Olden's book it emerges that the Weimar Republic died of its own faults and internal weakness:

... we went on playing at being a Republic —

democracy, parliament, free Press, social reform. There were a good few amongst us Germans quite aware that democracy, republic, social reform, extension of the rights of the individual, pacifism, and all the rest of it, was only play-acting for a period of uncertain duration, that the State had no real substantial existence, because the weapons were in the hands of its foes.

To-day there is no possible return to German Liberalism or to the now equally defunct Moderate Socialism. The horrors of Nazism must be extinguished and the force behind it must be broken, but that force is in the German nation.

The most tragic aspect of the present catastrophe is perhaps this: that had the other nations, and especially the Western Powers, shown sufficient wisdom, energy, and skill to contain the German eruption for one generation, Hitler and the Nazis might themselves have most effectively achieved the task of breaking that other, truly dangerous, Germany. For a new generation educated under these masters would probably have had no longer even the technical ability to try to reverse the verdict of the First World War. Then no amount of fanatical, hysterical Hitler-cult would have mattered, nor the publicity given to him abroad. " Hitler struts about in jack-boots ", " Hitler gazes at the mountains ", " Hitler greeted by blonde maidens ", " Hitler welcomes Lord —— at the Nüremberg Rally " — would have become innocuous captions in illustrated papers. It is the fatal combination, in democratic countries, of sentimental pacifisms on the Left with pro-Fascist leanings on the Right which has enabled Germany to get so far towards the goal common to the overwhelming majority of " Aryan " Germans.

III. BOTH SLAVES AND MASTERS

(" *Time and Tide* ", *July* 5, 1941)

A letter in *Time and Tide* of May 24, referring to my article on " Names and Realities " in its preceding number, speaks of " the two fatal extremes in Germany — a too submissive and deferential attitude on the part of the under-dog, and the love of power and a ruthless and tyrannical use of it on the part of the top-dog ". This view of the Germans, which is widely held, is based on accurate but superficial observation, and in distinguishing sharply between the willing slave and the ruthless bully, establishes a misleading, and potentially dangerous, dichotomy; these are not two mutually exclusive types, but two facets of the German character, closely interconnected, indeed inseparable, complementing and reinforcing each other; and on their combination is built up the Prussian State and the German nation. In the Prussian State machine everyone is both slave and master, be he a particle, a small cog, or a vital part; but whether insignificant or important, he is part of it, consciously identified with it, and sharing in its power and achievements. The men subjected to the iron discipline willingly accept it for the sake of that joint performance, and the less personal life and freedom the German enjoys, the more important it is for him to feel a member of a master nation, of a *Herrenvolk*. This is his compensation: even the most submissive and deferential of Germans partakes in the ruthless tyranny exercised by his State and nation at home and abroad.

On the other hand, the typical Prussian, however highly placed, looks upon himself as a servant of the State. When he commands, he does so on behalf of some entity superior to himself — which enhances his inborn brutality and ruthlessness. King Frederick William I, the father of Frederick the Great, was in many ways the prototype of the modern Prussian, and his son, who lived at first in mortal fear and hatred of him, finished by identifying himself with his father, and by taking a vow that, when king, he would sign no order without asking himself whether Frederick William would have done it; and Frederick II himself has become the idol of generations of Prussians, indeed of the entire German nation. Frederick William was a beast and a tyrant, who in wild paroxysms of fury would beat his children and his subjects and shout that they must love him; he came within an ace of executing his son, but finally contented himself with a primitive, savage expiation — Frederick's friend, Katte, was beheaded before Frederick's eyes. Still, that monster was an efficient, conscientious, hard-working, ascetic ruler, with a peculiar religion and morality of his own. Here is the description given of him by the distinguished French historian Lavisse:

> Frederick William had but few ideas, and those of a rudimentary kind: that a king, to be strong, needed a good army; that a good army had to be paid; that to pay it, money was required. Besides, he had a rare and original idea of his own

position: the King of Prussia was to him an ideal and eternal being, of whom he, Frederick William, was but a servant: " I am Commander-in Chief, and Minister of Finance to the King of Prussia ". The practical result of this mystical conception was that he did not allow himself to enjoy royalty: he was its gerent on behalf of a master; and all his life he worked under the eye of a master whom he knew to be formidable.

It is the lack of moral courage, self-assurance, and independence in the individual German which makes him seek safety, self-assertion, and superlative power in and through his State and nation, and which makes him glorify them beyond all bounds of sense and reason. Finding in them the desired compensation, he serves them with a patience and devotion such as more individualistic races find it difficult to muster and maintain, except in times of acute crisis. The German possesses an infinite capacity for group integration, and thus integrated is still capable of remarkable individual performance (which renders his totalitarian organisation extremely formidable). He loves uniformity, organisation, and hierarchy, which protect him from moral doubts and fear; and thus fortified, he makes an excellent workman, official, and even commander. His neatness, " sense of duty " (*Pflichtgefühl*), accuracy, indeed pedantry, are notorious: they are obsessionist and coloured with anxiety, not born of spiritual freedom. He wants to live *eine geordnete Existenz* — a well-regulated life, under orders. A friend of mine, while gate-crashing in the park of a German luxury hotel, was rudely accosted by a gardener who had spotted him as an intruder; with admirable presence of mind and understanding of the German character, he sharply replied: "Should anyone ask you what I am doing here, you will say that you don't know." "Yes, sir," answered the German, and walked off satisfied — suddenly burdened with the responsibility for my friend's presence he felt relieved when given a clear order. The Germans are temperamentally unfit for revolution: the Nazis did not proclaim a "revolution" until they had become possessed of the authority of the State; and one of the chief leaders of the German Social Democrats, when asked in exile why the working classes had not resisted, replied that the fault was his — he had not given the order at the right moment!

As members of a group-personality most people enjoy greater freedom from moral scruples and inhibitions, and readily do things which they would hesitate to do for their own benefit: which provides much of the attraction of politics and war. Machiavelli's doctrine, or the French *raison d'État*, justified a disregard of moral principles in the interest of the State. But it is the Germans, from Hegel and Fichte down to Treitschke and the Nazis, who have deified the State and nation; of this the ultimate expression is Hitler's maxim that whatever benefits the German nation is morally good and just.

The outlook and ideas of the modern supernationalists, their self-adoration, self-praise, and their pseudo-science, are very largely of German origin. No other people operates with its national label quite as naively and as persistently as the Germans, "*deutsch*" standing necessarily for something supreme and unique. They rattle off in their rhapsodies: "*deutsche Treue*", "*deutsche Wissenschaft*", "*deutsche Arbeit*", "*deutsche Wälder*", "*deutsche Eichen*" — as if no one but they had any conception of virtue, science, or labour, and no other country grew forests or oaks. Group-integration of the German type postulates uniformity, and self-adoration through the group justifies intolerance; to brook diversity, still more to esteem it, is to feed doubt and to induce corrosion. Hence the dislike which the most typical Germans at all times evinced for the critical, restless Jews in their midst, a dislike which in the Nazis has risen to a frenzy; and the disapproval and envy which the disciplined Germans feel for the easy-going Anglo-Saxons with their individualism and their sense of humour. To vanquish the Anglo-Saxons would be the supreme triumph which the German slave nation could achieve through its master State. That State has to be omnipotent to justify itself.

It is this which explains the sudden collapse in 1918, and the moral *débâcle* which followed on defeat. Doubt concerning the gerents of the German State who incarnate its power, concerning their efficiency, their knowledge of what they want and their capacity to achieve it, shakes the entire structure of the German nation and its discipline. Human beings can go on, wounded, maimed, battered; but remove a cog from a perfect machine and it is dismantled. This is the great weakness of Germany, which an obvious defeat would undoubtedly expose once more. Another weakness is in the changes which the post-war period and the Nazi régime have worked in the German character and in the

German State. Some of the Prussian characteristics survive: but there is a curious new infusion. Defeat and inflation have had a deeply unsettling and demoralising effect, and Nazi revivalism has assumed hysterical, egotistic forms alien to the old Prussian State. The army leaders are still always mainly Prussians, the political leaders are from Austria, Bavaria, and the Rhineland. The Prussian machine under non-Prussian leadership presents additional danger: for others and for itself.

"IN TIMES OF CONFUSION"

("*The New Statesman*", March 16, 1918)

[I look back twenty-four years: after the Treaty of Brest-Litovsk had been signed, I wrote the article reproduced below. I felt that the end had been reached of the early, naively idealistic, humanitarian period of the Russian Revolution, which had its counter-part in the opening stages of the French Revolution (but was to have none in those of the Fascists and Nazis). I was convinced that though Russia's power "may be eclipsed for years", it "can never be broken"; I foresaw that if the Soviets build up their military power, "Russia will be worshipped once more"; and about "the impervious Teutonic skull" and its emanations, I held the same views in 1918 as in 1910, and as I hold in 1942. Still, the mere pleasure of having been right would not make me republish the article (the only one in this volume written before the outbreak of the present war): but I think that it may be found interesting and useful as showing how at that critical juncture, twenty-four years ago, things appeared to a more or less impartial student of politics. Pro-Russian and anti-German, a Conservative by instinct, predilections, and doubts, but not from material interests or from fear — in short, a Tory Radical — I carefully watched the Russian Revolution without being affected by the hysterics which drove certain types of Conservatives into the dangerous absurdities of a home and foreign policy dominated by the fear of Soviet Russia. I did not believe in a "change of heart" in the Germans, and agreed with the view which the French and Poles took of them: but it seemed to me stark lunacy to attempt a settlement of Europe against both Germany and Russia — to proscribe them both, to despoil Russia of White and Little Russian provinces, to draw round her "*un cordon sanitaire*", and thus to create a common interest between her and Germany. Who in Western Europe were the foremost promoters of that anti-Russian policy? Those who are now the " men of Vichy ": in them " collaboration " with Germany is logical, and would have been good policy in 1919 — except that then they were inflated with victory. And what was the essence of their bitterest complaints against Russia? That she had repudiated her debts, and deserted her allies. Even for this purpose I reproduce this article: to contrast Russia's " betrayal " of 1918 with that of Vichy.]

"At the close of 1611", recounts one of Russia's greatest modern historians, Kluchevski, " the Muscovite Empire presented a spectacle of universal and complete disruption. The Poles had taken Smolensk . . . the Swedes had occupied Novgorod . . . the second false Dimitri had been murdered and succeeded, in Pskov, by a third pretender . . . the first expeditionary force of the provincial nobility had been broken up near Moscow. Meanwhile the country lacked an administration . . . the State changed into a kind of amorphous, coagulated federation." " On all sides the State of Muscovy is now torn by foes ", wrote in 1612 the boyars of Moscow in a circular letter to the towns. " In the eyes of all rulers round about are we now fallen into contumely and reproach."

The evil days have returned, and after having grown outwardly into the greatest Power on the European Continent, Russia has to suffer humiliation and disruption once more, because her inner structure was unsound and collapsed in an hour of crisis. She lies prostrate to-day, confounded though immortal. For the power of Russia, a nation of more than one hundred million men, united in speech, feeling, and thought, may be eclipsed for years, but can never be broken. She has to suffer now for all her past, for the crimes committed against her peasant nation, for the age-long sufferings which they had borne far too patiently, for their final rising, for the deep, mystic idealism of her Revolution, for its self-sacrifice as well as for its blunders, for all that is best in her, and also for the lack of understanding shown to her in the hour of trial by the civilised European world. Materialism incarnate strikes at Russia, and she sinks almost without a sound.

There were men who believed that powers not of this world would fight in defence of the nation which carried to the world what it conceived as the glad tidings of a new resurrection. Were these men dreamers? So far ideas have not proved a sufficient arm against guns and the impervious Teutonic skull. Russia " had snatched at heaven's flame " and tried to " kindle nations ".

> She was weak.
> Frail sister of her heroic prototype,
> The Man; for sacrifice unripe,
> She too must fill a vulture's beak.

The revolutionary Government has, in Lenin's words, " to submit to a distressing peace " — " the Germans have their knees on our chest ". Revolutionaries have to learn the bitter lesson of force. Lenin, the clearest thinker among the Bolsheviks, had foreseen it and had protested against the heroic madness of the last appeal for right and justice which Russia made at Brest-Litovsk in defence of others. With an inhuman touch he now describes the illusions of those who had thought like Trotsky as "revolutionary cant" and taunts them with a "craving for effect and brilliance". "To refuse to sign these terms is only possible to those who are intoxicated by revolutionary phrases." Obviously one may blow trumpets before Jericho, but one should not feel astonished if walls do not collapse, for things do not usually happen like that in the world. Lenin speaks about the necessity for "organised work" and "the creation of a mighty national army". Revolutionary militarism? Another phase of the Russian Revolution has come to an end. If the Revolution survives, it will carry the sword to the world. Then Russia will be worshipped once more. Men will say like Lucius Aurelius Cotta, the deeply cultured, cynical Roman official in "*Thaïs,*" "*Moi-même j'ai quelque respect pour un culte désormais impérial*". But now they deride. "MM. Trotsky, Joffe, Kamenev, and comrades," writes a typical German, Herr Rotheit, in the *Deutsche Politik*, "entered the barracks at Brest-Litovsk, where the peace negotiations took place, feeling as if they mounted a platform from which to teach the Germans seated on the school bench ' to throw spears no more, but worship the gods of Bolshevism '. The part was untenable, for Might after all is something very real. Perhaps in a hundred thousand years the time may come when weakness will be glory and strength shame. We have not got so far yet, although all the enemies of Germany attempt by sophistry to bring about such a change of ideas and thus to readjust the world to their own pleasing. As long, however, as the ideas hold good which have existed since the world began, Germany, paying no heed to any such attempts, may exult in her strength."

It is useless to discuss the latest German peace terms to Russia in this connexion. There can be no real peace between Germany and the Russian Revolution, and the governors of Germany know full well that if the Revolution survives in Russia it will vanquish them in the end. In parts beyond the reach of their armies a new life will develop and new forces will arise. The Russian peasants' and workmen's republic may abstain from active propaganda in Central Europe, but the very existence of such a republic will be propaganda, and sooner or later the movement will spread into Germany itself. On the other hand, wherever the German armies advance into Russia, whatever parts of the country they occupy, they will have to wage a relentless war. The Germans will not be able to allow the peasants in Livonia or in the Government of Vitebsk to retain the land which had previously been the property of big landowners, and at the same time forbid any such encroachments in the neighbouring provinces of Courland or in the Government of Vilna merely because in 1917 the battle-front intervened between them. They will have to restore the estates to the nobility wherever their influence reaches, and then every peasant will understand why the German is his enemy, and why he has to fight the German. The peasant soldier who now refuses to continue the war at the front will resume it in his own village and with means which only the peasant knows. Let the Germans add fresh territories to their old conquests! They have now broken down the quarantine of the old front, and the "disease of Socialism", which they dread most, will spread to the West. The Germans have undertaken war against forces such as no Government has yet fought, against an idea which knows neither bounds, nor borders, nor race. Compared to the limited material means which are employed in ordinary warfare, these forces may be called supernatural. But it takes time before they can make themselves felt to the full. We have to wait patiently and watch.

When the Revolution broke out in Russia, it was hoped by many that it would electrify and vitalise the forces at the front and produce immediately the effects that revolution had produced in the France of 1792. But there were enormous differences between these two cases. The French Revolution had had three years to organise its country before war supervened, and then it was faced by badly organised, effete Powers fighting in a half-hearted manner. The Russian Revolution broke out after almost three years of desperate warfare, and was itself the result of complete disorganisation. The enemy it had to face was Germany, whose force even the best-organised Western Powers have so far not succeeded in breaking. The Russian Revolution started with an elemental breach of discipline and subordination in the Army. The deadly blow to Tsarism was not inflicted by educated men fully conscious of their aims, but by the vast illiterate masses of the peasant soldiers who were exasperated by the sufferings and slaughter of the past three years, during which, badly equipped, they had to fight against Germany's shining armour, sacrificed in vain by hundreds of thousands. Their revolt combined with

"IN TIMES OF CONFUSION"

the revolutionary labour movement in the cities and with the agrarian revolt in the villages, a revolt as old as serfdom and private ownership of land. By a natural process the direction of the entire combined movement devolved on the votaries of Socialist ideas. These were no schemers and intriguers seeking profit by means of *Realpolitik* and treason. Russia was not waging the war alone — it had been brought by it into the closest contact with other nations. In the spring of 1917 Russia could have obtained peace at a small expense to herself. But she refused to make peace except in conjunction with her Allies, and thought of a settlement in which even the German nation might be given a chance to join as a willing partner. This was the idea behind the proposed Stockholm Conference. Whether it could ever have had the desired effect and would have shaken the hold which the German Government has on the German people is another question.

The proposal was not accepted, and Kerensky tried to revive enthusiasm for war in the peasant masses. When he failed there was nothing left but either to make peace or to use the severest measures against the unwilling Russian soldiers — to whip them, to shoot them, to drive them into battle, to change them back into a mute machine without a will. Had this been tried — so the Government felt — the attempt would either have ended in disaster or a weapon would have been forged with which the generals of the *ancien régime* could have killed the Revolution, or at least the Social Revolution. In fact, the Revolution would have been killed automatically in the very act of coercing the masses. For these reasons even the moderate

"IN TIMES OF CONFUSION"

Socialists refused to apply the methods recommended by Kornilov; the Bolsheviks opposed them by force. And this is the only sense in which the Bolsheviks can be said to have purposely destroyed the Russian Army.

When, in November 1917, the Bolsheviks came into power, they could yet have concluded peace with the Central Powers on conditions not altogether disastrous, though no doubt much worse than those which could have been obtained six months earlier. Lenin advised them to do so. In his opinion it was Russia's first duty to save the revolutionary conquests at home. Only after having completed the work of internal reorganisation could she undertake a new crusade. The Bolshevik leaders who conducted the negotiations at Brest-Litovsk, on the other hand, reckoned that, while the negotiations were still carried on and protracted by them, they would be able to stir up revolution in Central Europe and carry their gospel immediately throughout the land.

They obviously miscalculated, and it is Germany's sword which now pierces the body of Russia. But may there not prove to be a miscalculation in the German move also?

"SURVEY OF INTERNATIONAL AFFAIRS, 1938"[1]

("The Nineteenth Century and After", March 1942)

I

ON the title-page of this book appears the motto:

> The Lord will only keep those who are resolved to stake their strength to the uttermost and to concentrate their will.—Dr. von Schuschnigg to the Austrian Bundestag, 24 February, 1938.

Brave words spoken about a fortnight after the hapless Schuschnigg had submitted to monstrous treatment at Berchtesgaden, and about a fortnight before he surrendered without resistance. The man, the time, the pronouncement, and the sequel — what a felicitous choice of a motto![2]

I turned to the chapter on "The Seizure of Austria by Germany", which forms the core of the book, Czechoslovakia being left over for a separate volume. Going through it, I felt as if I was once again driving in a peasant cart along an autumnal Ukrainian field-track: slow progress in sticky ground; the wheels creak and wobble, each moving in its own somewhat irrelevant fashion; frequent skids and loud splashes, and an occasional spill.

[1] Volume I, by Arnold J. Toynbee, Hon. D.Litt. Oxon., F.B.A., assisted by V. M. Boulter (Oxford University Press), 28s.

[2] The passage is not even accurately transcribed: see text of the speech on p. 199 — "to concentrate all their will".

"SURVEY OF INTERNATIONAL AFFAIRS, 1938"

On the first page of the chapter (p. 179 of the book):

> The forcible incorporation of a previously sovereign and independent German State into a Prussian-made German Empire was not without precedent; Saxony, Hanover, Kur-Hessen, Nassau, and Frankfurt had all suffered this fate in 1866. . . .

What! Saxony heading the list of the only four States annexed by Prussia, when even of the twenty-one survivors which joined Prussia in the North-German Confederation, Saxony alone preserved the outward forms of her army organisation? No! only a skid; she soon revives as "a constituent State".

On the next page a homily on Austria's "historic mission": after having served as shield to Western Christendom against assailants from the south-east,

> Austria had latterly come to serve as a channel for imparting the highest form of Western Civilization, in a Catholic and German version, to the imperfectly westernised or quite non-western peoples of the Middle and Lower Danube and the Upper Vistula basins.

Good German Counter-Reformation stuff, such as a Vienna official apologist might have written a hundred years ago. But what was Austria's "mission" in Prague after the White Mountain, in the Prague of John Huss? Or in Cracow? Is Western Hungary superior to the districts where Calvinism and Unitarianism survived under Turkish suzerainty? What has Vienna produced or transmitted in the "Catholic and German version" which is of transcendent value?

"SURVEY OF INTERNATIONAL AFFAIRS, 1938"

Now Austria cannot "look forward to playing either of these two familiar and honourable rôles", writes Dr. Toynbee. She could not act as bulwark, so he admits, where none is required:

> nor could Austria resume her modern task of educating South-Eastern Europe in the Catholic form of Western Civilization now that she herself had been forcibly incorporated into a Third German Reich. . . .

But where is such education needed, and from that source?

On p. 183:

> The Legitimist cause struck chords in almost all non-Nazi Austrian hearts because it was attached to a past to which most Austrians still looked back with a wistful regret.

Wishful thinking in London rather than "wistful regret" in Austria. Many of us over here would have favoured a restoration of monarchy in Austria (though not of an Austrian Empire) to close the door on the National Socialists; but monarchism was dead even in the rural districts of Austria: in a generation which knew not Francis Joseph.

On pp. 186-7, after a quotation from Herr von Neurath's speech of February 1, 1938:

> These comfortable words, however, were not borne out by the subsequent course of events. On the 4th February it was announced that Herr von Neurath was to be replaced at the Foreign Ministry by Herr von Ribbentrop, and on the 18th March, 1939, he was appointed to exercise,

at Prague, the office of *Reichsprotektor* over a
"Protectorate of Bohemia and Moravia" which
had been carved out of the corpse of Czechoslovakia by the German sword in an operation
which was as truly an act of war as the Franco-
Belgian military occupation of the Ruhrgebiet
had been in 1923.

What a sentence, what a comparison! The wheels
wobble in all directions — a skid, a splash, a spill.

On p. 213, having mentioned that on March 18,
in Vienna, " Herr Himmler laid a wreath on the grave
of Dr. Dollfuss's murderer, Otto Planetta ", Dr.
Toynbee remarks:

> This was the second time within twenty years
> that the murderer of an exalted representative of
> the Austrian state had been posthumously hon-
> oured by the political beneficiaries from his crime.
> At Serajevo on the 2nd February, 1930, a plaque
> had been unveiled by Serbian hands in honour
> of the Archduke Franz Ferdinand's murderer,
> Gavrilo Prinsep.

And again on p. 232:

> At Klagenfurt on the 24th July and at Vienna
> on the 25th, the fourth anniversary of the murder
> of Dr. Dollfuss was celebrated by ovations for
> his murderers. The celebrations at Gratz were
> graced by an oration from Herr Hitler's deputy,
> Herr Hess; in the celebrations at Vienna the
> Reichsdeutsch Nazi leaders of Greater Germany
> were conspicuous by their absence. At Vienna,
> on the 25th, plaques commemorating the mur-
> derers as patriots were unveiled, *more Serbico*, in

the square outside the former Austrian Bundes-
kanzlei in the Ballhausplatz.

To de-confuse this paragraph, for Graz read Klagenfurt: it was there that Hess delivered his eulogy
on the murderers in the presence of Bürckel, Seyss-
Inquart, and the seven Austrian Gauleiters. And
as the names of the murderers were again officially
honoured at the Nüremberg Rally, on September 6,
1938, anybody's absence from the Vienna ceremony,
the day after Klagenfurt, seems unimportant. But how
does the Serajevo ceremony compare with the National
Socialist celebrations? It was to have been attended by
representatives of various societies and authorities, but
these plans were countermanded by an official order:
no member of the Yugoslav Government was present.
Dr. Toynbee's gibe at the Serb nation is more than
gratuitous: it is misleading.

Along certain stretches of the road the cart makes
satisfactory progress, though the journey is seldom
interesting. A useful record is supplied of the events
culminating in Dr. von Schuschnigg's resignation on
March 11, and in Hitler's entry into Vienna on the
13th; also an analysis of some of the available material
and evidence. Unfortunately the record is sometimes
apt to change into a mere catalogue; and, in a manner
reminiscent of Uncle Joseph's instructive discourses in
The Wrong Box, the reader is told, with dates and detail,
how Hungary, Great Britain, Italy, Japan, Chile, Spain,
Turkey, Latvia, etc., dealt with the problem of their
diplomatic representation in Austria after March 12;
how in April the plebiscite vote was taken at Lüderitz
Bay, Bilbao, Victoria in Brazil, Burgas in Bulgaria, Rio

de Janeiro, Christobal, and Tilbury; etc. Sometimes the haphazard compilation of newspaper cuttings becomes too obvious. On p. 226: "The suicide of a Jewish lawyer in Vienna was reported on the 17th March". What! the *first* Jewish suicide on the sixth day of the Nazi régime? No: probably it owes its prominence to a cross-heading in the *Daily Mail*, though it was only one of many reported. Four lines further: "By the end of the first week of Nazi rule in Austria there was a daily death-roll of suicides . . ." Only "by the end"? Possibly a blurred echo from *The Times* of March 17 — "the roll of suicides . . . grows daily longer". Lastly: "The police return of the number of suicides in Vienna alone between the 12th and the 17th March amounted to nearly a hundred, with 17 suicides on the 17th as the highest figure for a single day". But if March 12–17 stands for five days, the daily average is almost 20, if for six, almost 17 — how then can 17 be "the highest figure for a single day"? Answer: this passage is inaccurately copied from *The Times* of March 24, where the period named is "between March 12 and 21". The last excerpt (with the further remark, omitted by Dr. Toynbee, that "these figures do not include some suicides which occurred in the suburbs") would suffice, but it should be added that the figures were anyhow incomplete: there never was in Austria a strict system of inquests, and the Nazis, eager to see Jews die, were even less concerned about the causes of their deaths. On p. 226: ". . . by the time that Austrian Jewry entered upon its first Sabbath under Nazi auspices on the evening of Friday the 25th March " — had the

Sabbath of March 18-19 escaped before the Nazis seized Austria? This is slovenly writing: "facts" are rattled off, pages are filled with them; they are not deemed intrinsically of sufficient importance to be given close thought and examination; still, it is hoped that, in their aggregate, they will supply a record and a picture: like stones dumped into Ukrainian mud to make a road. Whereas whatever is worth imparting to the reader should be stated with painstaking care. Moreover, imperfect acquaintance with Austria is sometimes noticeable: for instance, in the constant misspelling of Graz into "Gratz" — as if an expert on Scotland wrote "Edinborough"; or on p. 201: "Field-Marshal Jansa" — he was a "*Feldmarschalleutnant*", a rank three steps below Field-Marshal.

There is a well-known passage in Hitler's speech of February 20, 1938, in which, referring to Danzig, he praises Poland for respecting "*die nationalen Verhältnisse in diesem Staate*". This has been rightly translated in the British Blue Book of September 1939, and in the Polish White Book, as "the national conditions in this State". But Dr. Toynbee produces a new version: "the national connexions of this state". The word "*Verhältniss*" is very commonly used in German to denote an extra-marital intimate relationship, but Hitler did not refer to illicit political intercourse between Danzig and the Reich.

The patchwork gathered from newspapers and documents is over-painted with flowers of Dr. Toynbee's fancy and predilections. There is a reference to "Austria's hitherto charmingly diverse social landscape", but only formal information is supplied about the social and economic changes produced by the *Anschluss*, or about the impact of National Socialism on Vienna's intellectual life. More than one-sixth of the chapter is devoted to " The Impact of the Third Reich on the Catholic Church in the Ostmark " — no doubt an important subject, but not to the exclusion of others: Vienna's culture was largely non-Catholic. The whole is impregnated with a Habsburgite sham-romanticism, akin to the stale scent of a dud Jacobitism. " The lawful heir and claimant to the Hapsburg[1] throne " (p. 230) — " claimant " would suffice. " Since the decline of the Spanish Hapsburg Monarchy in the seventeenth century, the Danubian Hapsburg Monarchy has been the premier Catholic Power " — shades of Louis XIV and the two Napoleons! " Among the Catholic intelligentsia in the West, the Austria of Dr. Dollfuss and Dr. von Schuschnigg was extolled as the pattern of how a Catholic people ought to organise its political life in conformity with the general precepts given in Papal Encyclicals " (p. 243); but as these two men accepted also precepts from Mussolini, such exaggerated praise came largely from people with Fascist or semi-Fascist proclivities, and the generalisation hardly does justice to the " Catholic intelligentsia in the West ", to their intelligence and judgment.

II

I turn to the other subject in the *Survey* with which I can claim to be acquainted: to Mr. Beeley's chapter

---

[1] It is time to finish with " Hapsburg ": the bearers of a name must be allowed to decide how to spell it, and no Habsburg spells it with a " p ".

on "The Administration of the British Mandate for Palestine, 1938–9." This is a much more scholarly piece of work than Dr. Toynbee's — carefully written, well-informed, lucid and full about the transactions which it discusses, yet considerate in selecting them, and reassuring to the reader, for its slants are gentle and its twists discreet: it presents a naked body of facts, pleasingly posed and decked with garlands of fig-leaves. The features are faithfully rendered, but the photograph is re-touched. Things which might jar or offend are softened by a delicate distribution of lights and shadows, and an adjustment of emphasis. The story is told, and yet left untold.

Consider the picture which can be obtained by going back to the photographic plate. It is given here, more or less, in Mr. Beeley's own terms — only the "asides" in brackets are mine.

> In 1938 [writes Mr. Beeley] the territorial expansion of the Third Reich added to the force of the Jewish plea for a haven of refuge, while at the same time it made the British Government more sensitive to the opinion of their Arabic-speaking allies in the Eastern Mediterranean and the Middle East.

The Arab revolt now had for its object "not merely to challenge the authority of the mandatory Power but to supersede it", and by October "the civil administration, outside the Jewish areas and the larger towns, had been almost entirely paralysed"; "many Arabs began to envisage the possibility of driving the British out of Palestine, and . . . the rebels undertook their most daring exploit, the occupation of the Old City

"SURVEY OF INTERNATIONAL AFFAIRS, 1938"

of Jerusalem". But when the control passed to the military, its recapture "proved surprisingly simple". (Many things in this story are surprisingly simple or simply surprising.)

In July 1937 the British Government had accepted the partition scheme of the Peel Commission; the Arabs rejected it, and when in December 1937 the Woodhead Commission was appointed to work out its details, the terms of reference "seemed to suggest a waning enthusiasm for the project" (the Jews dubbed it "the Repeal Commission"). When its report was published on November 9, 1938, the Government "lost no time in deciding" that partition was "impracticable". Representatives of "the Palestinian Arabs and of neighbouring States" and of the Jewish Agency were now invited to London — "the novelty of the London conferences", admits Mr. Beeley, "arose from the fact that the Mandate had not admitted the status of the Arab people as a whole in the affairs of Palestine. . . ." In October the Iraqi Foreign Minister had visited London "to discuss 'several questions connected with Anglo-Iraqi co-operation'", and submitted proposals "for the pacification of Palestine".

> It was believed in Jewish quarters that these suggestions were not unconnected with the other matters under discussion; and that, at a moment when England was fully conscious, for the first time since 1918, of the danger of a European war, she would be strongly tempted to remove a source of friction with her Middle Eastern allies.

"Middle Eastern allies" meant Egypt and Iraq, and

the Arab delegations included Jamal Husseini, Ali Maher, Nuri-al-Said, etc. The " most universally accepted leader " of the Palestinian Arabs, " the Mufti of Jerusalem, was singled out by Mr. MacDonald as ' wholly unacceptable ' "; but Musa Bey al-Alami came as his " personal representative ", and the Mufti's " consent " was openly asked by the Arab Delegations on several occasions. (" Now I must consult my Mufti at No. 10 ", Mr. MacDonald is reported to have once jocularly remarked at this Tea Party in Wonderland.)

The Arab demands at the London Conferences involved the abrogation of the Mandate and the Balfour Declaration, and were based on alleged promises, foremost on the so-called McMahon Letters. An Anglo-Arab Committee was set up to examine them. The British representatives found " that on a proper construction of the Correspondence Palestine was in fact excluded " from its pledges; but the Committee further " considered certain subsequent events and documents which were regarded by one party or the other as likely to assist in its elucidation " (how the " elucidation " of a Correspondence not concerned with Palestine can affect British obligations in that country is not explained by the Committee, nor asked by Mr. Beeley; and one of the parties which selected the documents was the Arabs, and the other, representatives of a Government out to appease them). And here is Mr. Beeley's further account:

> The committee's terms of reference did not enable it to express an opinion on the proper interpretation of these documents, nor would it

have been easy to do so without surveying a very much wider field. But the committee placed on record an agreed conclusion as to their general significance which had an important bearing on the wider discussions of the London conferences.

In the opinion of the Committee it is . . . evident from these statements that His Majesty's Government were not free to dispose of Palestine without regard for the wishes and interests of the inhabitants of Palestine.

"The publication of the committee's report" (recording an unsolicited opinion for which they had not surveyed the field) "was . . . a minor victory for the Arab cause", and " the attitude of the mandatory Power to the Arab claims was slightly modified as a result of the committee's proceedings " (" as a result ", and only " slightly "?). The Jews complained that they were not heard on a matter which vitally affected their interests, especially when the committee exceeded its task, and also scrutinized the Balfour Declaration; that, for instance, the attitude of the Emir Feisul, representing at the Peace Conference the recipient of the McMahon Letters and of the " Hogarth message," was never considered [1]; and they argued that anyhow

[1] *The Times* commented on this point in a leading article on March 23, 1939: "One very relevant point which the British delegates might well have made has been strangely omitted from their statement of their case. . . . It is certainly strange that the Arab delegation to the Peace Conference led by Emir Feisal, as he then was, and including two of the Arab representatives who have been taking part in the proceedings of the Lord Chancellor's Committee [the Anglo-Arab Committee mentioned above], should have made no demand for Palestine before the Council of Five at Versailles, if they were then persuaded of the justice of the Arab claim to that region."

the Mandate would cancel earlier declarations and agreements not incorporated in it. (But the weak argue only for record.)

The final British "proposals for an agreed settlement" severely restricted sales of land to Jews; provided for a Jewish immigration of 75,000, after which further entry would require Arab consent (the Jews were not to exceed one-third of the population); and for the ultimate establishment of an independent State after a transitory period — though the termination of that period was implicitly made dependent on Jewish consent. The Jews refused to negotiate on a basis which, with regard to immigration, effected, in Mr. Beeley's own words, a "*volte-face*"; severed the Jewish nation as a whole from Palestine, by limiting the Jewish interest in it to those already settled there; discriminated between the rights of Jews and non-Jews in its land legislation; condemned the Jews once more to minority status, and subjected them to Arab rule (no paper safeguards hold against the inherent logic of a situation). But the Arabs, too, refused — mainly because they demanded a definite date for their "fully independent state", irrespective of Jewish consent. Thus ended the London Conferences: discussions were, however, continued with the Arab States in Cairo, without the Jews, but with the participation of Palestinian Arab delegates from Beyrout, *i.e.* from the Mufti. New concessions to the Arabs followed: a wide and growing share in the administration of Palestine was promised as soon as order was "sufficiently restored", the stipulation about Jewish consent disappeared, and the British Government alone was to decide whether full independence should come at the end of five years.

The White Paper was issued on May 17. Mr. Beeley (after an amazing " black-out " to which I shall return) carries it straight to the Arab Higher Committee, the Zionist Congress, and the Permanent Mandates Commission. At Geneva Mr. MacDonald " sought to show that the policy announced in May 1939 was both compatible with the Mandate and consistent with the policies pursued by previous British Governments ", but claimed that new light was thrown by the " Hogarth message " on long-disputed phrases in the Mandate and the Balfour Declaration.

> The Chairman of the Commission, however, took the view that the Hogarth message, an assurance given by Great Britain to a third party and not communicated to the League before the Mandate was confirmed, could have no bearing on the Mandate, which was an international convention between the British Government and the League of Nations.

To cut the story short — the Mandates Commission unanimously declared that

> the policy set out in the White Paper was not in accordance with the interpretation which, in agreement with the mandatory Power and the Council, the Commission had placed upon the Palestine mandate.

Moreover, by four votes to three, the Commission went even further and declared that the White Paper could not be squared with the Mandate. Mr. Beeley emphasises that " it was a bare majority ", refrains from

"SURVEY OF INTERNATIONAL AFFAIRS, 1938"

stating what the other three said, and obliquely animadverts on the four (see p. 479, *n*. 2).

Now enter the photographic studio and look! On the side of the face away from the camera there is a nasty scar. What is it? The White Paper was debated in the House of Commons on May 22–23, and again on July 20, 1939. Mr. Beeley's chapter covers sixty-five pages: the Woodhead Commission fills ten, the Palestine Conferences fourteen, Arab Congresses four, the Zionist Congress of August 1939 three pages. And the British Parliament? When the Zionist Congress expressed appreciation of the attitude of " leading members of all parties in the British Parliament ", the reader learns, for the first time, from a footnote, that " the White Paper had met with considerable opposition when it was debated in the House of Commons on the 23rd May " (what about the 22nd?), and was " approved by an unconvincing majority ". Nothing more, not a word of what was said. Was it unimportant? Mr. Churchill described the new immigration laws as "a breach and repudiation of the Balfour Declaration ", a " new and sudden default ", " a one-sided denunciation of an engagement " — " there is the end of the vision, of the hope, of the dream ". Mr. Amery said that he could never hold up his head again if he voted for what he had deemed inconceivable, " namely, that any British Government would ever go back upon the pledge given not only to Jews but to the whole civilised world when it assumed the Mandate ". Mr. Herbert Morrison called the White Paper " a cynical breach of pledges ". Sir Archibald Sinclair,

Mr. Tom Williams, and many others, spoke in the same sense. About the Hogarth message and its " new light " even Sir Thomas Inskip said, when winding up for the Government: " It is not of sufficient importance . . . to spend much time on it ". In spite of a three-line whip the Government majority sank from a usual 220 to 89 — even Ministers abstained from voting. What is the use of an account which has no use for these men and their views? Whence Mr. Beeley's reticence?

Some of Mr. Beeley's most artistic touches require too much technical explanation to be dealt with here — *e.g.*, how on pp. 423 and 463 he treats Mr. MacDonald's violation of his own White Paper in July 1939. I shall discuss them elsewhere, and now limit myself to a few examples of Mr. Beeley's notion of even-handed justice.

> The replacement of selected by unselected immigrants could hardly have been agreeable to the Jewish Agency. But its attitude, after the publication of the White Paper, was curiously similar to that of the Arab Higher Committee in 1936 ; it maintained that illegal action was an inevitable consequence of the Government's policy, and declined either to co-operate in enforcing the immigration laws or to be made responsible for their breakdown (p. 423).

The Higher Arab Committee would not condemn a murder campaign, which indeed its head, the Mufti, encouraged or even directed; the Jewish Agency would not condemn or hunt down Jewish refugees who fled to Palestine from Nazi horrors. Exactly on all fours. Well done, Mr. Beeley!

"SURVEY OF INTERNATIONAL AFFAIRS, 1938"

About the Palestine Conferences, on p. 455:

> The efforts of the British representatives to secure some abatement of the original demands respectively put forward by Jamal Efendi al-Husayni and Dr. Weizmann met with no appreciable success.

Jamal Husseini demanded from H.M. Government the abrogation of the Mandate under which they hold Palestine; Dr. Weizmann asked for its continued application as it had been interpreted by H.M. Government and the League for seventeen years: how appropriate to bracket them together!

Another comparison, on p. 446: having admitted "the novelty" of introducing the Arab States into Palestinian affairs, Mr. Beeley writes:

> The mandatory Power might justify its summoning to London of Arab representatives from neighbouring countries on the ground that they were in reality as deeply concerned with the problem as were the Jews of Rumania or of the United States of America.

The Mandate guarantees rights in Palestine to the Jews of the Dispersion, and to the Arab inhabitants of Palestine. The Jews of Rumania are therefore an interested party under the Mandate, but the Arabs of Iraq are not. Indeed, on two occasions, in September and October 1938, Mr. Malcolm MacDonald himself volunteered to Dr. Weizmann the remark that the Arab States had no *locus standi* in Palestinian affairs, and when on December 14, 1938, in presence of

Dr. Weizmann, I reminded him of it, he admitted the accuracy of my statement.

The average reader having finished Mr. Beeley's chapter will sit back pensive but content, and say: "This is a difficult and complicated question. There are two sides to it. Much can be said on either side. We shall be blamed by both. But we must hold the scales even. I don't envy anyone who has to deal with this appalling problem."

III

Some of the other chapters in this *Survey* seem to me better than the two which I have reviewed — not only because I know less about their subject matter. Still, the weakest links determine the strength of a chain, and test the soundness of a system.

Although a note in the fly-leaf of the *Survey* describes opinions expressed in it as "purely individual", the book is issued under the auspices of the Royal Institute of International Affairs, a body which, in its own field, holds a unique position in this country. Whatever the present editorial arrangements may be, they do not ensure a standard of scholarly accuracy and impartiality worthy of the imprint which the work bears. Could not panels of experts, picked from among members of the Institute, read the proofs, correct mistakes, and question, for the final decision of a strong editorial committee, opinions which may appear to them biased or one-sided? Had the chapter on Austria been seen by such men as Dr. Seton-Watson or Mr. Wickham Steed, not one of the mistakes of fact pointed out above, nor of those which I had to leave

"SURVEY OF INTERNATIONAL AFFAIRS, 1938"

unmentioned, is likely to have survived. As it is, the *Survey* is as dull as a reference book, suffers from the defects inherent in collective works, and occasionally shows a lack of balance and an irresponsibility which would call for censure in an individual author, and are intolerable in a book published under the auspices of a Royal Institute.

THE JEWS

(" *The Nineteenth Century and After*", *November* 1941)

Who is a Jew? For large numbers of Gentiles, anyone whom they want to belittle or stigmatise. This type of Gentile, conscious of the slur which he puts upon our name, has in the past devised for us compassionate euphemisms, especially numerous in Continental languages: " Israelites ", " Hebrews ", " Old Testamentarians ", etc. Now the Nazis have invented " honorary Aryans " and, if it suits them, they allow a half-Jew with a Jewish father to establish his fitness for an honourable career by " proving " that, before he was born in wedlock (maybe half a century ago), his mother had committed adultery with an " Aryan ". Lueger, the Jew-baiting Bürgermeister of Vienna, and Field-Marshal Goering are both credited with the saying: " It is for me to determine who is a Jew ".

Whom are we Jews to consider a Jew? A prominent Zionist once remarked that, seeing how hard is the lot of the Jew, he accepts as such, without further question, anybody who claims to be one. On the Day of Atonement, before the most solemn prayer, the Kol Nidre, is said for those who have forsworn themselves, the Elders of the synagogue step forward and announce that these may re-enter and pray. At the hour of Israel's reunion with his God, there can be no enquiry into the past, no reproach, and no exclusion. And now in our history has come the Day of Atonement and the hour of the Kol Nidre. Those who were weak, or vain, or cowardly, or merely oblivious, who sought to evade sharing our common burden, and tried to forget and make others forget that they were Jews, or at least attempted to compromise with their Judaism and not be compromised by it, must be allowed to seek mental peace and moral comfort in a return to their God and to their nation. No other peace and comfort is the portion of any of us in the Dispersion.

In most countries some Jews have been allowed, at one period of history or another, under this or that garb, to rise to the highest offices and honours, to attain rank and power: as individuals, not as Jews. Yet there has hardly been one among them who at some stage in his career did not feel, closing on him and enveloping him, the miasmatic, choking film of that mysterious, undefinable " Jewish problem ", so unlike anything his neighbours have to encounter; and who then did not wish it were given to him to live the life of a humble but normal human being, about whom no one " wonders " and has doubts, and who is not asked unanswerable questions. And the Jew is lucky if these are merely " questions " and not charges, imputations, invectives — the efflux of the non-Jew's neurotic imagination or wrought-up temper. The more the Jew explains, the greater the anger and suspicions of the non-Jew: for the one does not know what to ask, nor the other what to answer. It is the " Third Degree " drawn out through the ages, insidious and yet devoid of conscious purpose.

In the country where the Jews are given the fairest

deal, in Great Britain (and the same applied to some extent to France before her defeat), they have a chance, but not always an equal chance, of doing work: and for whatever good work they accomplish they receive credit. But if a Jew errs, or merely incurs unpopularity, a resentment rises against him far more violent and venomous than were he a non-Jew. Edwin Montagu's Indian policy having displeased many Conservatives, his dismissal brought on in the House of Commons a scene of savage delight betokening a virulent anger such as has never been kindled by the numerous non-Jews who have bungled along the same path. Nor would in France the hatred even against a Socialist Prime Minister have risen to such fatal heights had not Blum been a Jew — the slogan of the Right Wing defeatists, " rather Hitler than Blum ", expressed more than mere loathing of Socialism. And what ineffable bitterness there is in the remark said to have been made in the hour of defeat by Mandel, the Minister who never wavered, that he could save France if only his name was Dupont! It seems doubtful whether " Rima ", or any other work of Epstein, would have evoked such strident, and sometimes even defacing, dissent had his name been Evans. Many of us are happy to acknowledge the eminently fair treatment which we and our work have received in this country. Still, in every one of us there is, deep down, the consciousness that we cannot afford to slip: a fall for us is harder and more irretrievable than for a non-Jew.

Not even in this country does the Jew enjoy the same moral freedom to express his views, especially in politics, as the non-Jew. If a Socialist, he is suspect of Bolshevism; if a Conservative, he is a " bloated capitalist ". Certainly not every non-Jew feels that way, and of those who do, few will show it: for Englishmen hate being unfair or rude. But there is seldom a cloudless sky over the Jew — as he speaks, shadows pass across, and feelings are aroused which, though rarely fixed in words, are present and real. Occasionally they find vent in an invitation to the Jew " to go back to his own country " — as if he had in the Diaspora a country which was his own and which would welcome him. When Sir Alfred Mond once advocated in the Commons Empire migration, which in any non-Jew would have been an irreproachable subject, a member of the extreme Left hurled at him the reply that it was not for a German Jew to tell Scotsmen to leave their country. When, some time in 1937, I defended the Treaty of Versailles in the presence of a certain Left Wing intellectual, he very nearly screamed at me that after all the years which I had lived in this country I was a complete foreigner, for every Englishman knew that it was " a bad treaty "; and when I said that we ought to have checked Hitler at an earlier stage by a preventive war, he replied: " I am a 100 per cent Aryan — what would you say if I justified Hitler's conduct as making preventive war against the Jews? " This man is not an anti-Semite; he has helped Jewish refugees; he is, in fact, a League of Nations internationalist; but feeling irritated at a Jew who happens to be a Conservative, he talked as a Fascist would to a Jew of the Left.

No doubt the fact that many of us are newcomers or the children of immigrants, have foreign names and foreign accents, adds to the difficulties, dislikes, and friction; but the "native-born" Jews of so-called "old lineage" grossly deceive themselves if they think that were it not for those "strangers" they would be looked upon as indistinguishable from other Englishmen. Every Jew must have come here at one time or another: and even in America the Jews are the only ones who cannot claim to have come over on the *Mayflower* — we miss every boat, and all the waters are to us "rivers of Babylon". We shift about in the Diaspora, driven by grievous disappointments, if not by downright persecutions and by bitter need; and our movements add to the discomfort of those who moved before us. The game of musical chairs goes on, the pace quickens till it becomes a breathless, giddy gyration, a dizzy round, a maelstrom. Polish Jews in Russia, Russian Jews in Poland, Polish Jews in Germany, German Jews in England, every kind of Jew in America — this merry-go-round of would-be-redeeming migrations changes in time into a wheel on which we are broken. For in the Exile the Jews are truly at rest only there where "the prisoners are at ease together" and "hear not the voice of the oppressor".

A man, to attain full moral stature and intellectual poise, to enjoy life and be socially creative, has to be at ease: this is seldom given to Jews who try to overcome the Galuth (Exile) by both accepting and denying it. While suffering slurs, often hard to define but always implying inferiority, they try to make themselves and others believe that relations are satisfactory, indeed normal. Such a Jew will tell you that he for one has never experienced any "discrimination", that he is treated by the Gentiles exactly as if he was one of them; he seems to take pride in it, and receives as a boon what normal people assume to be their birthright. A Scotsman with whom I had only a very superficial acquaintance, on my telling him that I was a Jew, said: " I do not know how you will like what I am going to say, but you are the first Jew I ever liked." I replied: " Would it interest you to know whether I like Scotsmen? " He admitted that it would not. " Then why do you expect me to be interested in what you feel about Jews? " He saw the point, as will any sane non-Jew to whom it is put. But when making his remark — not in the best taste — he probably expected me to be both flattered and hurt, to make excuses for the Jews which would be self-accusations and set him in judgment over us. To most people it is pleasing to establish their superiority and then to be censorious, indulgent, open-minded, and unconvinced. This is the game to which Jews submit when they worry too much about what non-Jews think of us: it is difficult to endure it with dignity, and to pass through it unscathed. The Jews have suffered the most incredible persecutions and tortures in the two thousand years of Dispersion. But so long as they remain a coherent, self-contained community, with a consciousness and a national pride of their own, they preserve their strength and vitality: and contempt or insults from their neighbours do not affect them any more than, say, those of eighteenth-century Chinese would have affected Englishmen resident among them. It was the semi-toleration accepted by the assimilated Jews which turned so many of them into neurotics.

THE JEWS

Every man carries in him and with him a communal memory and inheritance, the more distinctive the longer the conscious life of his race. Ours is the longest continuous history, most varied on the surface, least varied at its core, unique in character. On the rock of our existence, the Book, other nations have built, while we in the Dispersion have had to enter their abodes, adopting their languages, undergoing their influence, fitting ourselves into their modes of living, working within frameworks set to us by them; dissolving all the time, and yet surviving. Because of that " remnant ", people ask why the Jews do not dissolve? They might as well ask why glaciers do not melt? Every glacier melts in parts, at given seasons; and some have disappeared altogether; but to a certain type of intelligence, the glacier which is not, and the glacier which is, equally demonstrate the fact that glaciers do not melt. In the present world there is not enough warmth to melt down all the glaciers, nor to absorb even those Jews who would wish to be absorbed. For such there must be, at all times and in all countries: in the circumstances of the Dispersion, assimilation is a natural process, and those who succumb to it are neither the worst, nor necessarily the weakest; we all undergo assimilation in some measure or other; but those who long to be joined to their neighbours closer than they are, are the most unhappy among the Jews. For the desire to be " assimilated " is a confession of inferiority, an attempt to divest oneself of one's own inheritance in order to share in that of others. He who does that submits, without the will or means to stand up for himself, to the scrutiny and judgment of people for whom he feels attachment and an often uncritical admiration, but who do not necessarily feel any for him.

What a life, to be continually on trial and under examination! Uncertainty breeds anxiety, and anxiety provokes critical attention. Cold eyes glance furtively at the unwanted Jew; his presence produces subdued alertness; even if there is no open hostility, there is a more than ordinary readiness to find fault; the less people are willing to admit prejudice, the more eager they subconsciously are to justify it (and prejudice is the universal attitude of men towards strangers not strong enough to command their respect and approval). Speak out, and there is nothing more to be said: suppress things, and you cause discomfort and irritation. Most of the peculiarities with which the Jew is taunted (and sometimes tainted) are the result of deeper *malaise*. Harried, he is blamed for being restless; kept out or kept down, he is described as pushing and assertive; hurt, he searches for compensations and is called vain, blatant, or self-indulgent; insecure, he yearns for standing, power, and wealth: which sometimes protect him, but more often expose him the more to attack. Even in the most ordinary intercourse, uncertainty is apt to react unfavourably on his bearing. He is too eager to please, too affable, perhaps too intimate; too intent and emphatic; he shows off and talks too much — in short, he is self-conscious and embarrassed, and his company becomes exhausting. In public life he is too patriotic and public-spirited (for he continually pays entrance fees and ransom); or, having experienced social injustice, he becomes the spokesman of the injured and aggrieved — a part we have often played, and for which we have almost invariably paid the penalty.

At present the Jew is, if not a " refugee ", at least a perpetual evacuee from a non-existing home. Great numbers of Britons have in this war learnt how it tastes to be an evacuee; yet much greater numbers learnt how evacuees, even of one's own race, appear to half-willing hosts — " them evacuees (a nasty, crafty-looking lot) ", says Nathaniel Gubbins in the *Sunday Express*, speaking with the unmistakable voice of Everyman. And there is a phantasy of his which comes to my mind as I write about the Jew " on trial and under examination ".

> The Dog and The Cat had grown so big and The Man and The Woman had shrunk so small that it was The Dog who was taking The Man to the local Man Show . . .

Dog and Cat were discussing the peculiarities of the human breed, while The Cat was grooming The Man for the Show.

> The Man, bored and irritated, escaped The Cat for a moment and ran to The Dog. . . .
> " Come here, sir," said The Cat.
> " Never mind, Mansy Boy," said The Dog, patting The Man's head. " It'll soon be over."

If only the Jews could for once grow so big, be so firmly rooted in the soil, feel so perfectly at ease, and the non-Jews find themselves, by some miracle, circumstanced as the Jews are at present! The decent Jews would then befriend them, and occasionally lecture them in a kindly manner; and the nasty ones would indulge in spiteful criticism; and together they would, having become " Gentile-conscious ", analyse " Gentile peculiarities " and discuss " the Gentile problem ". I wish Nathaniel Gubbins would develop this theme; it would make people laugh, and some might stop and consider.

While emotionally the would-be assimilated suffer most, we are all in some degree assimilated to our neighbours, and dependent on them. As between individuals, I could ask the Scotsman why he expected me to be interested in what he felt about the Jews when he was not interested in what I felt about the Scots; but in the mass, so long as we retain any interest in life, we must care about those who can render it tolerable for us, or intolerable. I eschew speaking here of countries where the flood of anti-Semitism has broken all dams, where insulting the Jew is the law of the land, and killing him no longer murder, where the Jews are robbed of their possessions, debarred from earning a living, and finally herded together in overcrowded ghettos to await a slow, lingering death from starvation, exhaustion, and disease. I eschew speaking even of milder forms of anti-Semitic action, such as prevailed in pre-war Poland or Rumania. I speak of countries where the Jews experience nothing worse than discreet relegation or special advertency, and suffer of *malaise* and not of persecution; where the Jews congratulate themselves on their luck, and the non-Jews on their generosity; but where, none the less, anti-Semitism is like a dark cloud on the horizon, and friends come to the Jew with worried faces to tell him how much they are disturbed by the rapid growth of anti-Semitism which they have noticed recently. And this is usually said with a faint suggestion that the Jew can, and should, do something about it; although he can do about as much to deal with the rising storm, if it does rise, as men in a foundering barque can to assuage a raging sea. Had France in 1918 suffered defeat, and not Germany, new Déroulèdes and Drumonts would have arisen, and not Hitler.

Every nation keeps its own ledger; ours alone is kept by strangers, who place the achievements of individual Jews to their own credit, and leave us only with the debit side. And there is a vague belief in the Gentile mind that all Jews are marvellously knit together: therefore in some way responsible for every single one among them. If Smith operates in the " black market ", Smith does it; if Cohen, it is the Jew. Whenever some specially unpleasant or provoking incident occurs, Jews, who by no stretch of imagination could be connected with it, murmur: " I hope to God the fellow is not a Jew." When Hitler imposed a fantastic fine on an already ruined German Jewry because one young Jew, driven mad by the sufferings inflicted on his parents, had killed a German diplomat, he merely condensed and exhibited in hideous, grotesque exaggeration (as he so often does) an idea deeply ingrained and widely diffused among the Gentiles. Without the least power to control individual members of our race, who frequently have lost all touch with us, we are expected to achieve in discipline what a totalitarian dictatorship could hardly undertake. On the other hand, the merit and achievements of individual Jews are not as a rule reflected in the Gentile attitude to Jewry. When a non-Jew starts, " I have many friends among the Jews ", the Jew knows that this is not a preface to compliments: that a " but " will inevitably follow, leading up to anti-Semitic, or at least to highly critical, remarks.

A book could be written on the bitter absurdities of the treatment accorded to the Jews; another, proving that they themselves are largely responsible for the treatment they receive; and a third, to show that, seeing the conditions under which the Jews are made to live, they have preserved a remarkable and very creditable measure of sanity and decency. But the obvious conclusion of it all is that a situation which produces such results should not be continued indefinitely. Anti-Semitism did not start with Hitler, nor will it end with him: but it has been a trump card in his hand, as in the hands of innumerable smaller demagogues and scoundrels. In the interest both of the Jews and the non-Jews the ground must be cleared at last. But this will not be done by " seven maids with seven mops ", were they to sweep for a century.

The " emancipation " movement of the " assimilationists " arose in the individualist era; it knew only Jews, but no Jewish nation. Its leaders, rich and educated, had entered Gentile society, and approached the problem of their own people internally in terms of " philanthropy ", externally in terms of " toleration ". They planned to re-shape the lives of millions while treating them as so many individuals — an impossible task. At the same time, they wished to preserve the existence of Jewish communities: there was a duality of purpose resulting in an unstable compromise. They believed, and wished others to believe, that a national religious tradition and separate racial identity need not interfere with absorption by other nations. More logical were those who attempted amalgamation: but even this, as a mass movement, merely produces Marranos or " non-Aryan Christians ". Those who treat the Jewish problem as the sum-total of innumerable individual problems, render it insoluble; for each individual case is troublesome, and their aggregate unbearable. Moreover, the other nations do not cease to sense the Jews as a people apart, and express it in their exaggerated belief in Jewish " oneness "; but the Jews who, by reducing themselves to the level of a nondescript, a-historic group, cast away the dignity of a nation, court and incur indignities. For a sense of grandeur men derive only from the conscious collectivity — the nation. The greatness of a nation raises the status of its members; but the merit and achievements of individual Jews now lack the framework which would give them their full value. The first step towards a solution of the Jewish problem is for us to recover our historic national consciousness; then, and then only, can we expect the non-Jews to count with us. A nation is not a mere sum-total of the individuals who compose it; it transcends them all, and possesses weight and values which none of them can claim individually.

Every creature leaves its trail on the face of the globe, and every star affects the orbits of the other stars. Not one nation, however insignificant, can without distortion be omitted from the world's history: but remove the Jews and history becomes incomprehensible. We enter into everything that has happened in the last two thousand years, in which history was made by the interplay between creeds of Hebraic origin and the nations affected by them. Whether " the tables were the work of God, and the writing was the writing of God ", or whether they were the work of the People; whether the Sermon on the Mount was spoken by the Son of God, or by a son of the People: these events occurred in our midst, are part of our history, have determined our fate, and through us the fate of the world. Nineteen centuries ago our people divided: one branch, the Hebrew Nazarenes, carried into the world our national faith coupled with their new tidings, the other, as a closed community, preserved the old tradition. Yet both were part of one nation, and both are part of our national history. Only by seeing them as one whole shall we recover the full sense and greatness of our history. Those who went into the ways of the Gentiles, have permeated and transformed the heritage of other nations, and transmitted to them a creed which guides and binds, is cherished or endured. The others became the " remnant " which awaits the Return " that they may live ". The relation of men to every creed has been mixed in character; the highest intensity produces a polarity of feelings — love tinged with hatred. How much of the hatred which turned against the Jewish remnant was hostility to Christianity, diverted against those among whom it had originated? At last in our time, enemies have arisen to the Jews, the worst we ever had, conscious of that connexion. The Nazis started with an onslaught against the Jews, and part of Hitler's success was due to the widespread — often only half-avowed, half-conscious — sympathy which there was for that onslaught among all the nations. Sincere Christians never felt it, and were among the first to see the true face of Nazism; which by now is openly turned against Christianity and all its values.

Hitler will be defeated: and yet, unless the Jewish problem is faced in the light of history and with a courageous, realistic approach, it will continue to poison our lives and the minds of non-Jews. Normality must be our aim: to be no longer either " prodigies " or outcasts, or both. Jews with a national consciousness and purpose must be given an honest chance to build on the foundations which they have laid in Palestine: a Jewish National State must arise there once more (and then, after we have ceased to be a " peculiar people ", even the position of those who remain in the Dispersion will become more normal). There must be a country where Jews can live, work, and amuse themselves as they please; be good, bad, great, or ridiculous: but, like all nations, among themselves, not under the eyes of strangers. What otherwise the outcome of the Return will be, is beside the point. Some Zionists occasionally engage in high-minded, highfalutin discourses about the " magnificent contribution which we shall then be enabled to make to the common stock of humanity " — and demonstrate therein once more the Galuth mentality of men who feel beholden to pay tribute, for which they seek compensation in high-brow superiorities. If, having concluded the Great Journey, we shall become altogether humdrum and mediocre, that, too, will be our own affair: but our children will have a better life — and this suffices. No nation need justify itself in its own home, and it matters little what nations think of each other. " The political body has no heart . . ." wrote an anonymous Irish pamphleteer in 1779, " and nations have affections for themselves, though they have none for each other. . . . There is no such thing as political humanity." Scattered groups without a centre must not be exposed to the impact of nations. National emancipation is the meaning and essence of Zionism.

NUMBERS AND EXODUS

("*The New Judæa*", February–March 1942)

I

MANY years ago a little girl of about five used occasionally to invade my study and ask to be told stories. One day, when she placed herself too near to the open grate, I told her about another little girl whose frock caught fire; and there were only children in the house, who could not save her. "By the time Mummy came home the poor child was dead." "Tell me another story," said Molly. "No, now you tell me one," I replied. Then she told me back the same tale, but concluded: "By the time Mummy came home the poor child was dead; so Mummy spanked her and put her to bed."

When I hear people discuss post-war problems, I am frequently reminded of little Molly: they will name events in an inconsequential manner, and continue to think in terms of pre-war routine. There is a naive incomprehension, attachment to nostrums, and mental inertia; they look for repose where none awaits them, and talk wishfully about their own future and idly about that of others. How easily, in matters which neither grieve nor concern them, men are reassured or put off, especially if such prospects or doubts suit their own convenience. Explain to anyone, Jew or Gentile, who does not want the Jews in Palestine, that Palestine alone offers a solution of the Jewish question, and the answer is either that, once Hitler is defeated, the Jews will need no country of their own, or that Palestine is anyhow too small to satisfy their need, and that they must therefore look out for some other country — in short, they are offered " toleration " or " Timbuctoo ". But things are different for those who feel the burden and pain, who know the position, and will have to contend with it in the future. Politically and economically the Jewish problem is graver, but numerically smaller, than such anti-Zionists believe, or choose to believe. And the present anti-Semitic frenzy, which Hitler has raised as much as it has raised him, has wrought changes of which the implications can hardly be gauged as yet; but such is the destruction — moral, social, and physical — that it is no longer reasonable, or even possible, to discuss the Jewish fate and future in pre-war terms.

Numbers and distribution are the substratum of the problem, and have therefore to be considered first.[1] In 1880 world-Jewry numbered less than 8 millions; almost 6 millions, who spoke Yiddish, were gathered in the great Jewish Pale between Germany and Central Russia, the Baltic and the Black Sea, which comprised Poland, Lithuania, Latvia, White Russia, the Ukraine, Galicia, Rumania, and Northern Hungary; about 800,000 inhabited Central Europe,[2] 600,000 the Mohammedan East, while less than 600,000 were

---

[1] The figures in this essay are based on Dr. Ruppin's books, especially on the latest, *The Jewish Fate and Future*, published in 1940.

[2] In Central European Jewry, I include the Jews of Germany, German-Austria, the Czech provinces, and Switzerland; also part of Hungarian Jewry, which in Budapest approximated to the Central European type, while in the Carpathians and in Slovakia it remained East European.'

about equally divided between Western Europe and overseas countries.

Between 1880 and 1914 about 2½ million Jews migrated from the East-European Pale to the United States — the greatest Jewish mass-migration of modern times — and a few hundred thousand to South America, Great Britain, Canada, South Africa, and Australasia. This was essentially a " proletarian " migration. There was, however, another movement, very much smaller in size, but of great momentum : Jews mainly of the well-to-do and educated classes migrated from Bohemia, Moravia, Galicia, and also from Hungary, to Vienna; from Slovakia and the Carpathian districts to Budapest; from Prussian Poland to Berlin and to other German cities. Immigrants of this type entered Central Europe even across the Eastern frontiers, from Poland, Russia, and Rumania. During the four decades after 1871, *Mitteleuropa* — that Greater Germany which was not on the map between 1866 and 1938 — gained a very marked economic and intellectual preponderance in Eastern and South-Eastern Europe. The close affinities and connexions between the Yiddish-speaking Pale and the German-speaking Jewries were one of the factors which favoured in it the reception of Central European products, methods, and ideas. This material and cultural approximation in turn facilitated migrations: Jewish professional or business men of East-European extraction, educated and trained under the influence, or actually in the schools, of Central Europe, on settling there did not need to undergo readjustments and a re-education such as would have been required had they gone farther west. There was no loss of values, caste, or standing; on the contrary, the better economic and cultural conditions and the — at that time — more liberal atmosphere of Central Europe usually enabled them to rise in the social scale. Thus while before 1914 great masses of Jewish artisans or petty traders migrated overseas, Jewish wealth and intellect from the East-European Pale tended to concentrate in the capitals and cities of *Mitteleuropa*.

About 1900 world-Jewry approached 11 millions; almost 7 millions (less than two-thirds, as against three-fourths in 1880) lived in the East-European Pale; one million in Central, and half a million in Western Europe; and one million in the United States.

By 1914 mass-immigration raised that million in the United States to $2\frac{1}{2}$ millions. Elsewhere the increase was small; in the Pale it was checked by emigration, in Central Europe by a low birth-rate, by baptisms and mixed marriages (hence the great and growing numbers of " non-Aryan Christians "). In those years Central European Jewry reached its zenith: it comprised little more than one per cent of the population of " Greater Germany ", and less than one-twelfth of world-Jewry, but as at least three-fourths of the German-speaking Jews belonged to the educated classes, they counted for a great deal both in the countries of their residence and in the world-community of their own race. In 1914 Jews formed probably at least one-fifth of the intelligentsia in Greater Germany, while about half of the intelligentsia of world-Jewry spoke German. This led, outside Germany, to an exaggerated and misleading identification between Jews and Germans, and to a growing hostility against the Jews among the German upper and middle classes. For it is a woeful mistake to suppose that the educated are kinder or more tolerant: education creates vested interests, and renders the beneficiaries acutely jealous and very vocal.

War and defeat, loss of territory and currency inflation, affected the capitals and cities of Central Europe more than its rural and industrial districts: and therefore its Jews more than their Gentile fellow-citizens. Still worse was the physical destruction and economic ruin which befell the Jews of Eastern Europe: in the First World War all the fighting on the Eastern front occurred within the Jewish Pale, and it was followed by further local wars, civil wars, and by pogroms. Moreover, the disruption of the Habsburg Empire and the territorial losses suffered by Russia broke up the Pale and most seriously affected its economy. Its total Jewish population amounted in 1921 to over 6 millions — about 45 per cent of world-Jewry, as against 65 per cent in 1900 and 75 per cent in 1880. Two million Jews inhabited the parts of White Russia and the Ukraine which remained within the Soviet Union, besides some 700,000 in Central and Asiatic Russia — here they were not discriminated against, but, with the rest of the population, were virtually cut off from the outside world. Almost 3 millions were in Poland [1] — these suffered from the all-pervading anti-Semitism of an intensely nationalist régime and people, in an overcrowded and impoverished country;

[1] 2,830,000 Jews were enumerated at the Polish census of 1921. Their number was probably higher: a good many Jews, uncertain of their status and fearing expulsion, seem to have evaded the census.

some 800,000 were in Rumania, economically better off than in Poland, politically even worse; 250,000 in Lithuania and Latvia; and 200,000 in Slovakia and Carpatho-Russia.

During 1914–1919 there had been practically no emigration from the embattled regions of Europe; after 1919 the need for it, especially among the Jews, was greater than ever. But by 1921 the Jewish population of the United States had risen to about $3\frac{1}{2}$ millions, and restrictions of growing severity were enacted against immigration from Eastern and Southern Europe. In time, other overseas countries similarly closed their gates against East-European immigration. After 1930 there were only two important emigration movements from the *quondam* Jewish Pale: from its Russian part to Central Russia and Siberia; and from the States of East-Central Europe to Palestine — but since 1937 this, too, has been reduced to a ludicrously small size by regulations contrary to the Mandate. Thus, in spite of a now rapidly falling birth-rate, the Jewish population of Poland and Rumania continued to grow, in conditions which had already become politically and economically disastrous when the Hitler catastrophe broke over Central European Jewry.

Anti-Semitism has a long and ramified pedigree — *quae regio in terris nostri non plena doloris?* Yiddish, a language based on Middle High German and spoken in Eastern Europe, and " Spaniole ", a Castilian dialect used by Jews in the Southern Balkans and Asia Minor, bear witness to earlier persecutions and mass-expulsions. The Ukraine has an old tradition of anti-Jewish pogroms. And in the last fifty years Hitler has had a great many direct forerunners: the anti-Dreyfusards in France, the Christian-Socialists and Pan-Germans in Austria, Plehve and the "Black Hundreds" in Tsarist Russia, Dmowski and the National Democrats in Poland, the "Awakening Magyars" in Hungary, the various predecessors of the Iron Guard in Rumania, etc. None the less, it is no exaggeration to say that for a long time past anti-Semitism, and especially racial anti-Semitism, has derived its inspiration from German sources. More than forty years ago Anatole Leroy-Beaulieu described it in France as an importation from *d'outre Rhin*. In Tsarist Russia the German bureaucracy and the Baltic Germans were its foremost exponents. In Poland the worst anti-Semites were the German-trained Poles of the late Prussian provinces, although very few Jews were left in their part of the country. A great many of the "Awakening Magyars" (or at least their fathers) had German names. Throughout the world Jews and Germans had innumerable points of contact: and throughout the world the *Volksdeutsche* fomented anti-Semitism.

The defeat of 1918 seemed to have destroyed German primacy in Europe; and it greatly weakened the German-speaking Jewries: the threads between Central and East-Central Europe were breaking, while the English-speaking Jewries and the Hebrew Jewish National Home in Palestine were growing into new centres of world-Jewry. But the Jewish wealth and intellect of Greater Germany retained a good deal of weight: till the Nazis deliberately set out to destroy the Jewries in their midst, and even the "non-Aryan Christians". Numerically, the German-speaking Jewries had started declining even before the advent of Hitler: in the Reich their number fell from 565,000 in 1926 to 530,000 in 1933; in Austria, from 220,000 in 1923 to 180,000 in 1938. Within the frontiers which Greater Germany reached at Munich, there had been in 1933 some 750,000 Jews (besides the non-Aryan Christians). Of these, 350,000 emigrated before September 1, 1939; excess of deaths over births removed some 50,000; and about 350,000 were left under the Nazis. Even after the outbreak of war a certain number succeeded in emigrating; many more have perished, or have been deported to die in concentration camps and areas in Poland and France; by now less than 250,000 remain, mostly old, broken people. This is the end of Central European Jewry; it is not likely ever to be re-formed; and in another twenty or thirty years German will probably have disappeared as a language of any importance in Jewry (especially as Yiddish, too, is rapidly declining). Never since the expulsion from Spain and Portugal has there been so sudden and complete a ruin of a rich and highly educated Jewry.

The Nazi example stimulated anti-Jewish action in the legislation, and still more in the practice, of Poland, Rumania, Hungary, etc. Anti-Semitic feeling quickened, and anti-Semitic parties derived encouragement from what was happening in Germany; a systematic elimination of the Jews from the political, cultural, and economic life of those countries was demanded with ever-growing emphasis; the *numerus clausus* was to be applied against the Jews in education, professions, business, etc., and was to change in time — a short time — into a *numerus nullus*. In brief, there was to be an ultimate " evacuation " — enforced emigration — of the Jews. Hitler became the leader and pacemaker of the anti-Semites throughout East-Central and South-Eastern Europe, and even elsewhere.

In Western Europe (especially in England) and in America the anti-Jewish persecutions of the Nazis produced active sympathies for their victims — human and religious feelings, ethical and intellectual convictions, were outraged: refugees were received and befriended. But few people truly like strangers, and still rarer are those who do not weary of them. Moreover, the Central European refugees belonged almost all to the educated classes. The shadow of competition evoked vocal, even strident, reactions — it is easier to settle a hundred artisans than one doctor, intellectual, or factory manager. People were becoming " Jew-conscious "; and in the wake of the refugee victims the Nazis were spending millions of pounds on anti-Semitic propaganda: partly from an obsessionist spite, and partly because they saw their own advantage in it. They played effectively on widespread prejudices and gave them conscious expression. Warnings against Hitler could so easily be countered by being called " Jewish war-mongering "! And in every country the active pro-German groups found their staunchest adherents among the determined anti-Semites.

Throughout the world the Jews have suffered a most grievous loss of standing: for while sympathy (of limited duration) goes out to invalids or victims, only those possessed of effective strength are assured of respect. In the past the Jews were credited with great influence, even power — when in reality no people can be at all secure, still less strong, which is not master of its destiny through a State of its own. Hitler has shattered the legend of Jewish might. All that can be ascribed to us now, and that with impunity, is malignancy — like to medieval witches: who were burnt because they were helpless; had they been powerful, they would have been adored.

There remained one real escape and hope: the Jewish National Home in Palestine, where Jews were " of right and not on sufferance ", and which they entered under the Great Charter of the international Mandate. Their special relation to that country, based on the oldest, unbroken national and religious tradition, had been acknowledged; the dream of countless generations was to be realised in the hour of the greatest need. What Palestine now came to mean for Jewish self-respect and to tortured Jewish hearts and minds, few Gentiles will ever understand. (Why should they? it would require an effort seldom made on behalf of others.)

Still, even among the Nazis, some of the more honest and less obsessed showed at first a certain regard for Zionism. They would say to the Jews: " We do not acknowledge you as Germans; we do not want you in Germany. But we understand your nationalism and your desire to have a country of your own. We raise no difficulties against your going to Palestine." During the first years of the Hitler régime it was easier for German Jews to obtain exit permits and money transfers for Palestine than for any other country. But shortly the anti-Jewish activities of the Germans were to extend also to Palestine.

NUMBERS AND EXODUS

There had always been Arab hostility to the British Mandate and to the Jewish National Home; also pro-Arab sympathies and anti-Jewish feelings among the British officials. An attempt to crystallize and sterilize the National Home was made in 1929–1930: it was defeated by public opinion in this country and by a sense of international obligations. With the Abyssinian crisis a new element entered into the situation: Italy replied to British-sponsored sanctions by fostering Arab rebellion; Germany soon joined her in the game. From the outset great leniency was shown to the rebels by the Palestine Administration — it was the subject of comment by the Royal Commission (and of puzzled remarks by the military). But in 1938 the growth of the Nazi power and peril gave a further twist to the Palestine situation: the Jews, whatever was done to them, could not turn to Hitler; but the Arabs had to be " appeased ". They could now practise blackmail, and their friends render it effective. Mr. Malcolm MacDonald set out on his quest for a new righteousness; discoveries appeared like rabbits from a hat. The " Hogarth Message " of 1918, as vague as it was obscure, never communicated to Parliament, the League of Nations, or the Jews, never quoted even by the Arabs at the Peace Conference, at Geneva, or before the Royal Commission, was put into the scales against international treaties and an agreed practice of seventeen years. It was as if a husband, tired of his elderly wife, had conveniently remembered that he had committed a breach of promise before his marriage, and went to the law-courts to ask for its annulment. By 1939 the Jews had become helpless, and the consciences of the appeasers marvellously elastic: protests from Mr. Churchill, Mr. Amery, from Labour and the Liberals, were of no avail. The White Paper of 1939 condemned many tens of thousands, perhaps even hundreds of thousands, of Jews, who might have been saved, to slavery, torture, and death under the Nazis. During this war Poles, Yugoslavs, Greeks, etc., flying from the Nazis, were freely received in the mandated territory of the Jewish National Home: only not the Jews. That White Paper will disappear; but the human misery which it has helped to inflict cannot be undone.

"Darkness visible" was closing over the Jews as war approached. However great the changes in the distribution of Jewry had been in the last sixty years, very large numbers were certain to fall into the grip of the Germans: the Jews, therefore, more than anyone, dreaded this war, though no one did foresee how far Hitler's conquests would extend. On September 1, 1939, world-Jewry could be put at $16\tfrac{3}{4}$ millions. Nearly 5 millions were in the United States and Canada; half a million in all the other English-speaking countries; almost half a million in Palestine; and a similar number in South America: together $6\tfrac{1}{2}$ millions. Almost $3\tfrac{1}{4}$ millions were in Soviet Russia; over $3\tfrac{1}{4}$ millions in Poland; nearly $1\tfrac{1}{2}$ million in Slovakia, Carpatho-Russia, Hungary, and Rumania; a quarter-million in the Baltic States; together there were over 8 millions in Eastern Europe (less than 7 millions in the old Pale now forming only about 40 per cent of world-Jewry). Almost half a million remained in Central Europe (including the Czech provinces):

another half-million in Continental Western Europe; a third half-million in North Africa; a fourth, in the Southern Balkans and the Middle East (without Palestine). Adding to the $6\frac{1}{2}$ million Jews in the two Americas and the British Empire, those in unoccupied Russia, and some minor fragments, it will be found that only half of world-Jewry has escaped the Nazi clutches and now enjoys ordinary human rights; while the other half is, directly or indirectly, under German rule.

What it means for Jews to come under German rule requires little elaboration. They are singled out for concentration camps, and in those camps for torture and shooting. They are robbed of all their property, and of the means to earn a livelihood. They are immured in ghettos, where they die of starvation and diseases: probably one-fifth of the ghetto population will die in the course of a single year — and what a death! Moreover, the Germans and Rumanians advancing into Russia have massacred the Jews by the tens of thousands. Never has any European nation committed such mass-murders and atrocities. No one can forecast how many Jews in the Nazi-occupied territories, especially in Eastern Europe, will survive the war, and in what condition: speculations on this theme are as idle as they are gruesome. But what circumstances are likely to be for those who do survive should be considered even now.

Between September 1, 1939, and June 22, 1941, Russia occupied territories with a Jewish population, resident or refugee, of almost 2 millions. Where exactly Russia's frontier will be drawn after the war no one knows: but so much is certain, that some 4 to

5 million Jews will remain in Russia (I must, for the present, disregard losses through German mass-murders). Thus between 10 and 11 million Jews — roughly two-thirds of world-Jewry — will, at the end of the war, be in Anglo-Saxon countries and in Russia; and though it would certainly be too much to say that for these there will be no Jewish problem, its nature will be radically different from that which will arise for some $3\frac{1}{2}$ to 4 millions in Poland, Rumania, Hungary, Slovakia, etc. These will form the most immediate and most acutely urgent part of the post-war Jewish problem.

II

A hundred, or even fifty years ago, in a large part of the territories covered by the Jewish Pale, the classes into which society was stratified formed more than " Estates ": to be a gentleman, a peasant, or a Jew, denoted a nationality, a language, a religion, and a profession. It was so, for instance, in the vast regions which intervene between the frontier of ethnic Poland — roughly the " Curzon Line " — and the old frontier of 1772: most of the gentry spoke Polish, and were Roman Catholics; most of their peasants spoke White or Little Russian, and belonged to the Eastern Church; the Jews spoke Yiddish. Similarly in Slovakia and Carpatho-Russia, the gentry spoke Magyar, the peasants Slovak or Little Russian, and the Jews Yiddish. Practically all the commerce, big and small, in towns as well as in villages, was in Jewish hands; and so were most handicrafts. There were group-hostilities between Jews and Gentiles; there was little or no individual competition as between members of the same profession, nor group-ties, such as exist among the landed gentry or in peasantries (individual Jews who entered either class, as a rule, quickly ceased to be Jews). Even the rise of a large intelligentsia of a mixed character did not at first produce a sharp collision between Jews and Gentiles: the Christians filled the numerous posts in the Army and the Civil Service, the Jews filled the " liberal professions ": the magistrate or public health officer, for instance, would be a Gentile, the advocate or doctor in private practice a Jew. The Christian intelligentsia, descended largely from the smaller gentry, would hold something *de par le roi*, complete with uniform and rank, and akin to the Army; the Jews would be left the unprivileged part of the profession, akin to trade.

But in time agriculture and Government service no longer sufficed, and a strong Gentile influx into commerce, handicrafts, and the liberal professions, gave rise to a new, far more virulent, type of anti-Semitism. " Do not go to the Jews, but keep to your own kind " became the slogan of so-called " Christian "[1] merchants, shopkeepers, doctors, advocates, etc. The matter was raised to ideological levels: it was argued that the growth of a Polish, Magyar, Rumanian, Lithuanian, Slovak, Ukrainian, etc., middle-class was essential for the healthy, well-balanced development of

[1] On the European Continent, " Christian ", as an adjective, whether in the name of a political party or of a bank or shop, has almost invariably an anti-Jewish connotation. The story is told that when Dr. John Mott, of the Y.M.C.A., was introduced to Admiral Horthy, the Hungarian Regent expressed his great pleasure at meeting Mott, as he, too, was " at the head of an anti-Semitic organisation "!

the nation, that the towns as centres of political power and cultural influence had to be " de-Judaised ", and that it was therefore the duty of the nationally-minded to help to oust the Jews from the posts and professions they filled. This process was very much hastened during the twenty years between the two World Wars by the growth of "*étatisme*" in the new States: wherever a branch of trade or production, or any service, came under State control, the Jews were almost invariably eliminated. Now the Germans have set an example and new standards for the exclusion and spoliation of the Jews: the human right to individual property or to a share in public property, and the human claim to work and to a livelihood, no longer exist for them. In States adhering to the Axis — Slovakia, Rumania, Bulgaria, Vichy France, etc. — this process of economic and social extermination of the Jews has been carried out in a manner which would have seemed unthinkable ten, or even five, years ago; while the two million Jews in Poland, who came in 1939 under Nazi rule, have been expelled from innumerable villages and towns, and herded together, immured, in monster ghettos, having first been stripped of practically all their property. Attempts to leave these ghettos — be it by mothers in search of food for their children — are punished with death.

What is to happen at the end of the war? In Soviet Russia the surviving Jews may be re-absorbed, without difficulty or distinction, into the community of which they had formed an integral part. In countries such as France, Holland, also the Czech provinces, etc., where the elimination of the Jews, though advocated by certain parties, was not a widely accepted national programme, a considerable degree of restitution and reintegration will be possible. But what about East-Central Europe? There, too, restitution of rights and property seems the only just and decent solution. Equal citizen rights can be restored by legislative acts: but what will they amount to in practice? As for property, in Poland for instance, destruction, transformation, and transfers (and not of Jewish property only) have gone so far, and have been carried through on so vast a scale, that restitution may possibly have to come, to some extent at least, across wide measures of nationalisation. How will the Jew fare in such a re-settlement? And will it be possible to give back to him the place which he has filled as trader, artisan, or professional man in some town or village from which he has been removed by the Nazis? Even before he had been relegated to the ghetto, it had been the desire and endeavour of a very great number of his neighbours to squeeze him out — can he be replanted? What opposition and hatred would indiscriminate attempts of that kind provoke in East-Central Europe! What opportunities would they offer to Fascists and semi-Fascists in an atmosphere demoralised and brutalised beyond all description! They would be apt to poison from the outset the political life of those countries. Moreover the economic rehabilitation of those Jewries will require an enormous financial outlay: is it reasonable to spend vast resources on re-establishing Jews where they are not wanted, and whence a great many of them desire to emigrate? For had America and Palestine been wide open to Jewish immigration during the twenty years between the two World Wars, a very large proportion of the Jews of East-Central Europe would not be there any more.

It is better to face these facts now, and think of a sound and realistic solution. A programme of mass-evacuation, such as is demanded by the extreme anti-Semites, or advocated by the Revisionists, is wrong and immoral in principle, and impracticable. The Jews, many of whom have lived in those countries almost as long as (and sometimes longer than) their Gentile neighbours, cannot be expelled at will, against their own will; and even were they all anxious to go, a transfer of millions could not be effected in a couple of years. To lay down the programme of a short-term mass-evacuation of Jews from any part of the Pale is a dangerous piece of political charlatanry: it would merely supply anti-Semites with plausible excuses for " cold pogroms " against Jews unable to remove themselves as quickly as the anti-Semites would like, or against such as do not want to leave. A similar piece of charlatanry is the demand made by some Jewish " assimilationists ", in this country and in America, for an integral replanting of the Jews everywhere in East-Central Europe : behind this ingenious suggestion is the fear that if any difference is made between Jews and Gentiles anywhere, and if Jews are anywhere expected to emigrate, perhaps the idea might occur to anti-Semites in other countries to advocate an extension of this programme — and so such Western Jews choose to profess and postulate an impossible, nay disastrous, settlement for fellow-Jews who, after having suffered unspeakable tortures, deserve to have their fate and future considered on sound lines, and not merely to suit the supposed convenience, fancies, or fears of the " O.T.I." [1]

It is clear that at the end of this war there will have to be a very large, carefully planned Jewish emigration from East-Central Europe: it is equally clear that even one million cannot be removed within a year or two. But the mere existence and working of a sensible, large-scale emigration programme would take off the sharp edge of anti-Semitic movements in those countries, and enable responsible statesmen to attempt a moderate and regular solution of the Jewish problem. Try to settle a hundred thousand Jews on the land in Poland, where there is not enough room for those already engaged in agriculture, and you court disaster. But an attempt to train them on farms for emigration would meet with little opposition. The same will apply to other work, for which there will be plenty of scope at the end of the war. The greater part of the younger generation among the $3\frac{1}{2}$ to 4 million Jews of East-Central Europe will have to be removed; add to this few hundred thousand of a floating refugee and *nigré* population in other countries; lastly, a certain umber of Jews from countries where the Jewish roblem is not patently acute, but who desire to exhange the uncertain " toleration " of the Diaspora for a full and free national existence of their own: here is a problem of several millions to be resettled in one or two decades. It is, of course, impossible to attempt precise forecasts: for the scheme itself and the position

[1] These initials have nothing to do with Officers' Training — they stand for " Order of Trembling Israelites ".

of those concerned are bound to change in the process of its realisation. Its success — the rise of a Jewish national State and Commonwealth — is likely to improve the condition and standing of the Jews even in the Diaspora, and to diminish the material pressure inducing emigration: on the other hand it may, on grounds of an ideological character, induce emigration where it is not contemplated at present. The growth of a Jewish nation will undoubtedly lead in the Diaspora to a clear cleavage between those who want, and those who do not want, to be Jews: it will strengthen the Jewish national consciousness of some, and hasten integral assimilation of others, and normalise the position and status of both kinds. It will put an end to the " amphibious Jew ", the moral " *Luftmensch* " — a nondescript who lives in the air, and apparently on air.

Emigration, reintegration in a State and Commonwealth of our own — but where? For the national Jew there is only one answer: in Palestine. To offer us any other country is (to quote Mr. Ben-Gurion) like offering us a different religion: that other religion may be very fine and noble, but it is not ours, and we therefore do not want it. " Thus nature has made us ": we have adhered to our own religion for thousands of years, whatever price we had to pay for it; our religion is essentially national in character; and the core of both our religion and our nationalism has always been the return to the land which the Lord has given to us and to our fathers, from old and even for evermore. There have invariably been " flesh-potters " among us; there have always been those whose highest and only wisdom is to " serve the King of Babylon, and live ". But in this most terrible of all crises, compromises are breaking down. The stark absolute reasserts itself: and for us the one final and absolute goal is Palestine. There alone can we be reborn as a nation, and washed clean of all that the Exile has done to us. Those who feel thus, will accept no compromise; those who do not, will not succeed anywhere in establishing Jewish settlements, and securing our national, or even their own individual, future.

Many of us who had undergone assimilation have passed through a phase of what is called " territorialism ", repeating to ourselves: " We need no Holy Land; the land which will be ours will be holy to us ". Herzl, the founder of political Zionism, himself started with the idea of a Jewish State uncorrelated to Palestine, and partially relapsed into it when ready to entertain the Uganda offer of Mr. Joseph Chamberlain. But then he was a half-assimilated Central-European Jew whom the rising tide of anti-Semitism had cast back on to the Jewish shore — he was not rooted in a living Jewish community. The East-European Jews, even those of Kishinev who had just passed through a terrible pogrom, almost unanimously refused the Uganda substitute for Palestine. They spoke with the voice of believers. To gather in those who for thousands of years had been " tossed to and fro among all the kingdoms of the earth ", to re-form them into a people, to settle the oldest town-dwellers on the land that they may stay — requires more than the combined workings of distress and philanthropy. For countless generations we waited for the Messianic miracle to accomplish the Return: if it is to be achieved by the work of men, this must be done in the tradition and faith which have made us live and bid us survive. To find rest we have to go back to " the old paths, where is the good way, and walk therein "; elsewhere the earth is waste and void, and the heavens have no light.

There have been many attempts at settling Jews outside Palestine, some supported by a Government, like the schemes in the Crimea, the Ukraine, or Biro-Bidjan, others by powerful financial backing, like the work of the Jewish Colonisation Association in the Argentine: but in each case the results were disproportionately meagre. On the other hand, the Zionist work in Palestine was started with slender financial resources, and had to be carried on under an Administration which, for the most part, treated it with incomprehension or even hostility, or who, at the best, were what they called " neutral "; and yet such was the success that when circumstances gave the opponents of Zionism a practically free field, they had to resort to anti-Jewish discrimination and to prohibitions in order to arrest the most successful colonisation work of the last two decades. This was done at a time when Palestine had become for great masses of Jews the main refuge from Nazi tortures and semi-Nazi persecutions; and therefore, to soothe consciences and feelings, " territorialist " talk was revived — about Guiana, Alaska, San Domingo, Madagascar, North Australia, Kenya, etc. Or, to obviate criticism, the references were to some unnamed, undiscovered country — cheques drawn against non-existing funds. For where, outside Palestine, can room be found for settling very considerable numbers of Jews in search of a permanent home and of a national existence? The various tropical or arctic territories could, at the best, absorb insignificant driblets. The first prerequisite of any serious territorial scheme would be a fair-sized country available for white settlement; and then it would have to be seen whether the experiment (unsupported by the devotion and idealism which Palestine draws to itself) would be any more successful than were, for instance, the attempts to settle British ex-soldiers in Australia at the end of the last war. But anyhow, where is such land to be found? None of the countries of East-Central Europe, which now harbour the surplus Jewish population, can provide such territory — all these nations themselves feel greatly cramped within their borders. Russia may successfully re-absorb her own Jewish population, unsettled by the Nazis, but certainly has no reason gratuitously to enlarge her task and problem. It is idle to expect the United States, Canada, Australia, Brazil, or the Argentine, to open their gates to a large Jewish immigration: for even were one of these countries to set aside for the Jews some extensive stretch of White Man's Land (which none of them contemplates doing), unless it transformed that "reserve" into a concentration camp, there is every likelihood that these people, settled on soil to which they have no attachment, would drift into the towns and into their previous professions. That kind of "agricultural colonisation scheme" would prove in the end an excessively complicated and costly method of achieving what those countries definitely do not desire: a very considerable increase in their Jewish urban population. And yet the fact has to be faced that unless a sound scheme for Jewish emigration from East-Central Europe is devised, and implemented as part of the post-war settlement, the countries of that politically most inflammable area will be burdened with a deadly problem, and Western Europe and the overseas countries with an immigration pressure ten times greater than the Nazi régime had created during the years preceding the war.

At the end of the last war, the Jewish National Home in Palestine was looked upon as a dream to be tested by experiment; while an improvement of conditions in the Diaspora, in a world "rendered safe for democracy", was confidently expected. The Palestine experiment has proved feasible; the Jewish population has increased by more than 400,000, and the possibilities of colonisation, so far from being exhausted, have been shown capable of such further expansion as to provide room at least for the younger generation of Jews desiring to return to the National Home. Meantime in the Diaspora conditions steadily deteriorated, till the anti-Semitic fever reached a climax. The unsolved "Jewish question", a focussing point for passions and hatreds, helped to render the sick post-war world safe for demagogues — what anti-Semitism did for Hitler inside Germany, and outside, no other appeal could have done. How this came about, historians will have to explain; but to argue with mass-movements is to play the intellectual Canute. And even to enquire whether the reasons adduced are good or futile, serves no practical purpose: all human reasons are subjectively good, and most are objectively futile, but what matters is that people have them. Anti-Semitism may be an obsession, Jewish *malaise* an ailment, and Zionism a monomania: but the obsession and ailment are worldwide, and the monomania more than three thousand years old. Common sense and a certain measure of humility are essential ingredients of statesmanship; those who fool about with tides and mighty streams, or apply to them " White Papers " and Guianas, expose their own pitiful insufficiency. Hitler and the forces which have rallied to him have placed the Jewish question in the forefront of world-politics, and rendered it more acute than it had ever been. At the end of this war, at least two-thirds of world-Jewry, and possibly up to three-fourths, will be included in the two Anglo-Saxon Empires and Russia, and practically all the rest in countries which it will be incumbent on them to restore or to reorganise: the new distribution of Jewry and the responsibilities of victory will combine to make the Jewish problem the concern of these Powers, and an unsolved, envenomed Jewish problem in East-Central Europe will inevitably react on their own countries. Nor is it possible to crystallize or stabilize Palestine in its present condition: there are many millions of Jews who will never abandon the age-long goal of the Return, and the half-million in Palestine will never accept minority status in the National Home. The only way of forcing on us such abandonment and acceptance is by the Hitlerite method of extermination: all the ages bear witness that till our last breath we shall remember our God, our Land, and our People.

At the end of this war, nations will reap benefits and will have to make sacrifices: there will have to be give and take, and readjustments on a scale and of a character hardly ever attempted. Pettifogging casuistry, clever intrigues, and spiteful hatreds will not make history nor build up a new world. And it cannot be beyond the range of statesmanship to square the equation between the Arabs and the rest of the world which through Palestine alone can find a solution of the Jewish problem: national independence and unity within the vast Arab territories, and extensive help in developing them, must surely count as sufficient compensation for a strip of country the size of Wales which even now is bi-national, and is to the Jews the one and only place in the entire world which they claim as their national heritage.

To the assimilated Jews who have already found (or think that they have found) permanent homes, to these men " beyond Jordan ", the Zionist can say, in the words spoken by Joshua, when he addressed himself to the tribes already possessed of homes and land, that they, too, must help, for they will never truly settle down " until the Lord have given your brethren rest, as he hath given you, and they also have possessed the land which the Lord your God giveth them. . . ." And to those who stand between the Jews and Palestine, the Zionist addresses words which still resound after more than three thousand years: " Let my people go. . . ."

JUDAICA

(" *Zionist Review* ", *April* 18, *October* 17, *November* 7, *November* 21, 1941)

In 1921, on my first visit to Vienna after the war, I happened to engage in a discussion about Jewish Nationalism and Zionism with one of those high-minded, broad-minded, open-minded, shallow-minded Jews who prefer to call themselves anything rather than Jews. " First and foremost ", he declared in a pompous manner, " I am a human being ". I replied (and this was twenty years ago): " I, too, once thought so; but I have since discovered that all are agreed that I am a Jew, and not all that I am a human being. I have therefore come to consider myself first a Jew, and only in the second place a human being."

President Masaryk was one of the truest philo-Semites I ever knew; he did not believe the Jews to be cleverer than the non-Jews; he, for one, did not think us different from other human beings.

According to Aristotle, the " Stateless " must be a god or a beast; nowadays he is usually a Jew.

Overheard anywhere on the European Continent between 1919 and 1939:
" Look at this Jew! What did he do in the war? Some racketeering? "

" He was in the Army."

" Ye-e-s! Somewhere behind the lines."

" He served four years in the trenches."

" Well — even there he knew how to take care of himself. Why wasn't he wounded? "

" He was wounded several times."

" But so many of our best men were killed. Why is he alive? "

Indeed, why not cut the cackle by starting with the last question?

A. J. Nock, in his articles on " The Jewish Problem in America ", published in the *Atlantic Monthly*, quotes a friend as saying about the Jews: " They have got something which they don't need to tell one another, and they can't tell us ". What is it? Obviously a " *maase* " (a Jewish story); of which the definition is: " something every Jew has heard before, and no Gentile can understand ".

Sometimes I think that Zionism itself answers this definition: every Jew knows it, and hardly any non-Jew truly understands it.

In June 1940 I dined alone at a restaurant, and at the neighbouring table sat a Colonel wearing several ribbons of the last war, a Captain just returned from Dunkirk, and two ladies. The Colonel talked in so loud a voice that I could not help overhearing scraps of his conversation—possibly he wished it to be heard. " They call themselves Czechs, but they are all Germans." And next: " Two hundred yards from me lives a German Jew. I can't understand why the fellow is not interned. When the first Hun lands in this island, I shall shoot that Jew out of hand."

In the last war, a Jewish artist, with permission from the War Office, was making sketches at the front. He looked foreign. One day a Colonel found him at work.

" What are you doing here? " the Colonel asked sharply.

" Drawing your battery."

" Have you a permit? "

The artist fumbled in his pockets — no, he had left the permit at home.

" What is your name? " thundered the Colonel.

" Goldberg."

" Carry on, carry on," replied the Colonel, fully satisfied. " Had you said Smith, I should have put you under arrest." This Colonel had sense.

" Assimilation ", as the word indicates, is a halfway house. The true and clear alternatives are fusion or full and separate national existence. Both mean normalisation. The Irish in Great Britain, the United States, or Australia never feared lest an Irish State in Eire should render their position in these countries difficult or ambiguous. Only assimilated Jews entertain such fears.

The position of the Jews in the Diaspora will become easier once the Jews have attained full national existence in a Jewish State in Palestine. They will have attained equality with other nations. They will be able to live among these nations and preserve their nationality, as the Swiss usually do; or they may preserve merely a certain racial identity, as the Irish in Anglo-Saxon countries in which they are assimilated; or they may fuse completely, as the Huguenots have in this country.

But the real history of the Huguenots has never been written: how long they preserved their identity, intermarrying among themselves and maintaining in their Church a separate national character; how much they suffered, feeling uprooted and in a way *déclassé*; how the shadow of homelessness lay on them, sapping their vitality; how families, numerous at first, died out, or were reduced to very small numbers.

Shmarya Levin once said to President Masaryk: " The only Czechoslovaks are the Jews: everyone else is either a Czech or a Slovak." At the time of the last census I was staying in the house of a Scottish friend who, proudly but incorrectly, entered her nationality as " Scottish ". She was followed likewise by a Scottish guest. A " depressed " Englishman in protest entered himself as " English ". I alone put myself down as " British ", and could not have done otherwise had I wished to.

In May 1919 I had in Paris a long talk with Paderewski, then Polish Premier. The Jewish problem naturally figured largely in it.

" The Jews in England speak English," started off

Paderewski, " French in France, German in Germany. Why do they not speak Polish in Poland?"

" But do you want them to speak Polish? " I asked in reply.

" Of course I do."

" Please consider," I said. " In Germany the Jews form about one per cent in a highly educated population; and yet this has sufficed for them powerfully to influence German literature, science, the Press, and the theatre. If you want the Polish Jews, who form 10 per cent of the population, to give up Yiddish and learn Polish, you will have to educate them. And then *you* will have to adopt a different language if you want to think your own thoughts."

After a moment's reflection Paderewski said: " You may be right. But let them at least speak Hebrew and not Yiddish, which jars on us."

" As a Zionist I certainly should wish the Jews to adopt Hebrew," I replied. " But you must allow me to say that once you give up your demand that the Jews in Poland adopt Polish, what language they speak is an internal affair of ours."

A few days later, I met one of the leaders of the Polish Left, a fine and fair-minded man. " With us," he said, " one hardly ever mentions the Jews now without cursing." Still, he and his friends were prepared to stand up for Jewish rights — " but," he added, " then you must go with us." " Do what your conscience bids you," I replied, " but don't, on that basis, claim to mortgage our existence."

It is curious how often even upright men think that

doing justice to the Jews entitles them to levy, at least political, tribute.

Years ago I heard the son of a millionaire of Jewish extraction, in the presence of non-Jews, deny being a Jew. I replied: " As you aren't a Jew, let me explain to you something about my people. Like all nations, we have patricians and plebeians. The plebeians are ashamed of their origin." The non-Jews laughed.

Sir Lionel Abrahams, of the India Office, was an assimilated Jew with a warm feeling for Palestine. He told me that after the war he wrote to one of the most prominent opponents of Zionism: " I remember the feeling which my old grandfather had for Palestine. I also remember how in the 'eighties when Russian Jews were flying from pogroms, you and I, then young men, tried to establish some as pedlars in the City; they had no heart for the place, and they were not wanted there. On what grounds can we now refuse to help them when they wish to go to a country to which they feel deeply attached? " His friend replied: " You are too clever for me."

Shmarya Levin said to me: " Before 1914, a couple of million Jews went to America, a mighty stream; but each of them thought only about himself or his family. A few thousand went to Palestine, a mere trickle; but everyone of them was thinking about the future of our nation."

JUDAICA

The Balfour Declaration marks the end of the period of the " *shtadlonim* " (the Jewish oligarchs who spoke for Jewry on the strength of their wealth and their position in the Gentile world), and the beginning of democratic leadership in Jewish politics. Still, the Declaration was addressed to a Lord Rothschild — at that time Dr. Weizmann was not yet sufficiently prominent to be its immediate recipient — but the then Lord Rothschild, and still more Baron Edmond de Rothschild, were more than " *shtadlonim* ". The protest issued after the Balfour Declaration had been published will probably count in Jewish history as the dying speech of the " *shtadlonim* ".

A most generous American-Jewish millionaire, who was bitterly opposed to Zionism, once talked to me about our settlers as a " subsidised immigration ". I then showed him passages in James Truslow Adams' book, *The Founding of New England*, recounting how " the English-American balance-sheet showed a colossal amount spent in exploration and attempted development " against a handful of people settled in Virginia and Bermuda; how the London merchants, who backed the *Mayflower*, " received almost no interest upon their investment ", and soon came to see " that the principal itself was lost "; and how in spite of the enormous natural resources, the Colonies, short of capital, " borrowed heavily from England " till " the inherent unsoundness of the position ", concealed by continued immigration, became evident when that immigration stopped.

JUDAICA

Some years before I first visited Palestine, I spent a week-end with a well-known Colonial Governor. At dinner I talked enthusiastically about Palestine; next morning at breakfast, asked when I had been there last, I confessed that I had never been there.

"Then how can you be so enthusiastic about it?"

"And how could the Love of Zion have survived two thousand years of Dispersion," I replied, "if we were unable to feel it without having seen Palestine?"

In the Spring of 1929 I met a certain Palestine official who, in an aggressive manner — only too well known to us — began to enquire about Jewish colonisation in the Crimea (he was one of the well-wishers to Jews *in absentia*).

"There you get land free, whereas in Palestine you have to pay for it through the nose."

"Yes," I replied, "we have to pay for permission to drain marshes."

"And you spoil our duck-shooting."

I wonder what an Englishman would think if, say, an American made such a remark about England. But he was not the only one from whom I have heard it. I did not leave it unanswered.

"Anyhow," he said, "we have saved your throats from being cut."

"Leave our throats to ourselves; but when trouble comes, don't try to disarm us."

This was a few months before the disarming parade in Jerusalem.

JUDAICA

One of the better Palestine officials thus explained to me his preference for the Arabs: " When I go to an Arab village and give an order, they obey; in a Jewish village, they argue."

A very common attitude towards our work in Palestine is to pay it compliments, and then raise barriers against it; and tell us that we are so clever and persistent that we shall overcome them. The well-known maxim of the British Administration about " holding the scales even " in practice means " to make the obstacles to our work proportionate to our effort ".

Some Christians choose to lecture us for not being sufficiently pious in Palestine. Our ancestors placed their religion above all worldly considerations — but was the treatment meted out to them for it such as to entitle non-Jews to prescribe to us now what form our religion should take, and to pin us down to the traditional form for which these critics have developed so deep a respect? A story is told about the late Rabbi Kook which they had anyhow better ponder on before talking about this matter.

Some ultra-orthodox Jews came to Rabbi Kook, and accused the chalutzim of being " *epicorsim* " (" Epicureans ", *i.e.* irreligious). Rabbi Kook replied:
" When we had the Temple, no one was allowed to enter the Holy of Holies, except the High Priest; and even he only on the Day of Atonement, after prayers and ablutions. But when they were building the

Temple, any workman could enter it, dusty and dirty, at all times of the day and night. Keep silent — they are building the Temple."

During the exceptionally hot summer of 1911, a railway strike broke out in this country, and during the railway strike a small pogrom occurred in South Wales. It started at Tredegar, spread to Rhymney, Bargoed, etc. As soon as the train service was resumed I went down to see what had happened, and went the round of these mining villages. In one small place I went to the house of an ultra-orthodox rabbi; he kept me for a meal, but before we sat down I realised that I was in for some elaborate prayers. I had to explain to my host that, not having been brought up in the Jewish religion, I did not know our religious customs. He looked at me with real feeling, and said: "You have come to see what has happened to us. You have a good Jewish heart. That's all that matters."

I hope that man has lived to see the Jewish revival in Palestine, and that his honest Jewish heart and understanding will yet rejoice in the re-birth of a Jewish State.

When I was a boy, there was an old Jew on our estate in Eastern Europe who used to tell me stories about my ancestor, Eliyahu ben-Solomon, the Gaon of Vilna. The one which made the greatest impression on me was this:

About the middle of the eighteenth century a distinguished French Jew came all the way from Paris to Vilna to discuss the Law with the Gaon. On the third day of their discussions the Gaon said: " When we go back to Jerusalem . . ." The French Jew interrupted: " And if we do not? " The Gaon did not reply. He called his servants and told them to put his honoured guest into the pillory for twenty-four hours.

TWO BOOKS ON EASTERN EUROPE

I. THE UKRAINE

(" *The Times Literary Supplement* ", January 11, 1941)

A GREAT virtue and rare merit of Mr. Allen's new history of the Ukraine [1] is that its author, while dealing with the background to one of the most controversial political problems, and with its recent developments, has no axe to grind. This is an honest attempt at writing the history of the part of Southern Russia known as the Ukraine, and not propaganda. In fact, having studied carefully the 400 pages of Mr. Allen's book, the reader will be hard put to it to tell whether the author considers the " Ukrainians " to be a separate people or a branch of the Russian nation. That he should not have reached any definite conclusion on this point is evidence of knowledge and of prudence.[2]

[1] *The Ukraine: a History*, by W. E. D. Allen (Cambridge University Press: 21s.).

[2] The question whether the Ukrainians are a nation is frequently discussed as if it could be tested by historical argument or settled by theoretical disquisitions ; whereas not even the question whether Ukrainian is a language or a mere dialect, can be decided by such means. Dutch has separated from German, and Afrikaans from Dutch, while the German-Swiss, whose vernacular is incomprehensible to the ordinary German, employ, as a rule, German for their literary language. A dialect may become the literary language of those who use it in everyday intercourse, or it may not — and there is no predicating about it. Nor does a difference in literary language necessarily entail political separation, as the fanatics of sectarian nationalisms seem to assume. The fanciful rewriting of history, such as is often practised

But the fact that he does not even try to summarise the relevant material, is connected with a weak side of his work. It is almost throughout narrative, with little attempt at analysis.

Its first chapter on " The River World and the Kievan State (up to 1240) " is a fascinating account of the sudden growth of an early civilisation on the great river route " from the Varangians to the Greeks ", where in wide lands inhabited by Slavs, Finns, and Mongols, Scandinavian influences met and blended with those of Byzantium. Trade and the city-state flourished in Russia at a time when agriculture and feudalism prevailed in Western Europe. Novgorod arose in the north, and Kiev, " the mother of all the Russian towns ", in the south. There, in the midst of the virgin steppe, a court grew up, reproducing the refined, sophisticated, formal culture of the Byzantines. There was quick development, great splendour, the glow of a magnificent civilisation. But the end was near: the " meridial " connexion between the Baltic and the Black Sea was broken by successive blows delivered, across the steppe, by Altaian nomads moving in a " latitudinal " direction. The most celebrated epic of medieval Russia, " The Tale of Igor's Host ", deals with a campaign against the nomads.

Written at the end of the twelfth century, it reflects the dominant conception of its epoch — the unity of Russian lands. This theme lends by Ukrainian separatists or their interested backers on the Continent, is, therefore, both childish and futile: but it is apt to mislead foreign opinion, especially as the Russians — at times too strong to worry, at other times too weak to care — have hitherto refrained from arguing the case for Russian unity before foreign publics.

great pathos to the Tale. The unknown author urges all Russian princes to unite against the common enemy in the steppe. . . .

Even at this stage, Mr. Allen has to fend against certain strained " interpretations " by modern Ukrainian historians which " can only be considered as strongly biased and founded on misunderstanding and as making no contribution to historical truth ".

In the thirteenth century, the fertile lands of South Russia were reduced to a desert, a process to be repeated several times during the next four or five centuries. The population fled into the forest lands, north and west, and the metropolitan area of Kiev became a borderland — which is the meaning of the word " Ukraine ". The second chapter of Mr. Allen's book deals with " The Russo-Lithuanian State and the origins of the Ukrainian Question (1240–1569) ". In the fourteenth century, the Lithuanian princes tried to re-establish the meridial line from the Baltic to the Black Sea, and founded a state which was infinitely more Russian than Lithuanian.

> Gradually the Russian language became the official language of the administration and the law. Legislative acts, governmental edicts, were published in Russian. In the capital of Lithuania, at the court of the Lithuanian princes, Russian replaces the language of the dominating race.

During the next three centuries Lithuania's princes were to contend with those of Moscow for the leadership of all the Russias. But at the end of the fourteenth century an event occurred which complicated the situation: in the west, Lithuanians and Poles were engaged in a struggle against the Germans, and a dynastic connexion was now established between Poland and Lithuania, whose pagan princes, together with their own Lithuanian people, were converted to Rome, while the Russian provinces remained Greek-Orthodox. In the course of the next two centuries the relations between Poland and Lithuania — cultural, social, and political — were growing closer, though not without friction. Finally, in 1569, a constitutional Union was established, and the provinces south of the Pripet marshes, which form the bulk of what is now known as the Ukraine, were transferred to Poland, which since 1340 already held what is now known as East Galicia.

The next century is dealt with in Mr. Allen's third chapter on " *Rzecz Pospolita* and the Cossack Ukraine (1569–1654) ". The *Rzecz Pospolita* — the Republic of the Polish landed classes — was an amazing growth, of which the harvest and aftermath still cover the ground of a good part of Eastern Europe. A " nation " arose based not on race, language, or religion, but on class; the Polish nobility and the extremely numerous petty gentry cut themselves off from the Polish people, and to them were joined the landed classes of the Russo-Lithuanian provinces. A very large proportion of the families which now constitute the Polish aristocracy and gentry are of Lithuanian or of Russian and Greek-Orthodox extraction — the Radziwills, Sapiehas, Sanguszkos, Czartoryskis — to mention a few; similarly, Kościuszko, Mickiewicz, and Pilsudski are of White Russian or Lithuanian origin. All over the great expanse of the sixteenth-century *Rzecz Pospolita*, the upper classes were gradually succumbing to Polish and Roman Catholic influence, the transition from Lithuanian and Russian often going across Latin, the official and cultural language of the Republic, and from Greek-Orthodoxy across Protestantism, which gained great numbers of adherents among the upper classes; these, at the Counter-Reformation, became Roman Catholics. Moreover, there were systematic attempts at establishing a Uniat Church which would connect the remaining Greek-Orthodox nobility and gentry, and also the lower classes, with Rome and Poland, and separate them from Russia. The revolt which broke out in the Ukraine about the middle of the seventeenth century, and which marked the beginning of the downfall of the Polish Republic, had the double character of Greek-Orthodox opposition to Rome and Union, and of a revolt of free peasants, who in these wild border lands had the habit of arms, against the attempts to reduce them to serfdom. There is a peculiar type of free peasant in the south of Russia, with a Cossack tradition, which forms the core of "Ukrainianism"; this, to the present day, is a social and economic, much rather than a "national", movement. Whoever cuts across its path with a different code will meet with fierce opposition; national slogans, of whatever character, will be found no counter-weight to this peasant movement.

In the great rising of 1648–1654 the peasant masses under Cossack leadership proved their surprising, and in certain ways sinister, power — the massacres which ensued finding in Europe no parallel in savagery till Hitler's advent. By the Treaty of 1667, Poland retained the Ukraine west of the Dnieper except Kiev, which, with the eastern part, passed under Moscow; the south remained under Tartar-Turkish dominion. This settlement was further complicated by constant struggles between the peasantry and the Cossack Elders, who tried to step into the shoes of the defeated Polish big land-owners. The story of the endless intrigues and revolts, moves and counter-moves, is told in detail, sometimes in excessive detail, in the chapter on " The Ukraine of the Hetmans (1654–1709) " — though it is good to get at last the story of Mazeppa stripped of literary and operatic legend.

Surprisingly short and superficial is Mr. Allen's treatment of the next two centuries, down to 1914. Nineteenth-century developments in East Galicia are almost completely neglected, though it was there, under Roman Catholic Austrian and Polish dominion, that Ukrainian separatism was fostered and grew into a serious political movement. A certain amount of information is given about the Ukrainian movement in Russia, though even this is not systematically dealt with; for instance, there is next to nothing about the suppression of the Uniat Church, or about the remarkable ease with which this was achieved everywhere except in the Polonised districts. That Church, to the peasant masses, was Eastern in all its essentials; the Union, on the religious side, meant very little to the masses, while on the political side it was unpopular in the Russian Ukraine. Only in East Galicia, after the Uniat Church had become firmly intertwined with the Ukrainian separatist movement, did it strike deep roots.

The period of 1914–1939 in the Russian Ukraine is,

however, analysed with greater care, and the spurious, often farcical, character of the Ukrainian *Rada* and Directories is exposed. Vinnichenko, one of the chief leaders of the Ukrainian movement in the years 1917–1918, finished by admitting that " national questions at that time did not have the overwhelming importance which the Central *Rada* wished to ascribe to them", and that the *Rada* and its members were hated and laughed at by the population. " It was not they who elected us, but we who imposed ourselves on them." The moment the support of German bayonets was withdrawn, the Ukrainian Governments, whether *Rada* or Skoropadsky, collapsed. Similarly unsatisfactory was Pilsudski's experience with his Ukrainian protégé Petlyura; the Bolsheviks were able easily to defeat all these mushroom Governments. The book concludes with an interesting chapter on the economic history of the Ukraine, and with a postscript on the Ukraine and Europe, 1939–1940.

Mr. Allen's book, which is to be welcomed, is naturally not a piece of original research: it would be impossible for anyone to attempt it over so large an area and so long a period, especially with regard to a foreign country. But where good secondary sources are available, he has done the work, on the whole, in a satisfactory manner. His acquaintance with the Russian historical literature seems thorough, with the Ukrainian satisfactory, but with the Polish rather slight and superficial. Mistakes of an obvious kind suggest that his knowledge of Polish history has been acquired *ad hoc*, and is therefore apt at times to give out in a surprising manner.

TWO BOOKS ON EASTERN EUROPE

II. CARPATHO-RUSSIA

("*The Times Literary Supplement*", December 23, 1939)

Mr. Winch's *Republic for a Day* is a brilliant book [1] by a man who can see and can write, and enjoys doing both; who knows and understands a good deal, and yet refrains from discoursing too much; a man with wide interests and sympathies, but free of any purpose of his own — in short, an ideal eye-witness. Mr. Winch spent the first ten weeks of 1939 in that quaint strip of country on the southern slopes of the Carpathians previously known as Carpatho-Russia, then renamed "Carpatho-Ukraine" — a mere fringe, and a backward fringe, which, none the less, during that period was to reflect, in a manner not devoid of farce, movements and problems that beset whole worlds. The lower middle classes, intellectually half-baked and intoxicated, have entered active politics; and, infected with the virus of nationalism and " leadership ", they make life a misery for those who merely wish for a normal existence. In a drop of dew can be seen the colours of the sun, and this account of life and politics in a remote mountain community reflects the mental disturbances of untold millions of men all over Europe.

The muddle about the names tells part of the tale. The inhabitants of Carpatho-Russia have always called themselves " Ruski ", a designation used by the peasant population from Murmansk to Odessa, and from Brest-Litovsk to Vladivostok. Alien rulers called them " Ruthenes ". Now among them, as among their

[1] *Republic for a Day*, by Michael Winch (Hale: 12s. 6d.).

kinsmen in the adjoining provinces of East Galicia, the Bukovina, Bessarabia, and in the Russian Ukraine, one party considers the local tongue a mere dialect of Russian, while the other declares it to be a separate " Ukrainian " language. The Poles were of two minds about it: they favoured Ukrainian nationalism as a weapon against Russia, but combated it in East Galicia, where it was strongest, as they wished to Polonise that province. The Germans could turn Ukrainian nationalism both against Poland and against Russia, and in doing so Hitler pursued an old line of German policy. The Czechs, who in 1919 took over the government of this strip of Slav country freed from the Magyars, found it a ticklish job, and their oscillations between supporting the " Russians " and the " Ukrainians " may have been due to embarrassment as much as to policy. Ukrainianism is vociferous and seemingly progressive, and it has received indirect support from the fact that the Soviets have accepted the " Ukrainian " conception. The " Russian " creed is deeply rooted in peasant Conservatism, and in Carpatho-Russia it found expression in mass-conversions from the Ukrainian Uniate Church to Russian Greek-Orthodoxy — before 1918 there were only 12,000 Greek-Orthodox in a " Ruthene " population of about 400,000, now there are 150,000. As arbiters the Czechs could hardly have escaped unpopularity, but they apparently added to it by trying, in this chaos, to propagate their own language.

As a result they have left behind a fund of unpopularity in spite of all the honest work, good and plentiful, which they have done for the country. The twenty years of Czech rule " were good years," many peasants said to Mr. Winch, " and we all had work and bread." And this is from a talk which he had with a Jewish taxi-driver, whose statements are fully borne out by Mr. Winch's own observations:

> During the Czech period, the country had progressed three hundred per cent, he added. In the Hungarian times it had been a lost land. It was the Czechs who had put the roads in order, built the bridges, taught the people to read, put up hospitals and so forth. I asked him if he thought the peasants appreciated the work of the Czechs. He thought very few had an active appreciation of it, but that the majority of them were well content under the Czech rule and did not want to have anything to do with a new movement which threatened to upset it.

None the less, when evil days came for the Czech Republic, and Nazis, home-grown and imported, began to swarm in Carpatho-Russia, the one wish of a good many inhabitants was to get rid of the Czechs at any price, and they did not hesitate to enter into frenzied intrigues with the Nazis. Obviously one white race should not try to run the Government for another, nor waste its resources and energy on such work.

Mr. Winch brings out the attractive sides of the Ukrainian movement, but also its childish bombastic conceit, its imitations of Nazism, and its violence. From time to time he had to escape from that " enervating atmosphere of intrigue " by going up into the mountains, or at least to the (Czech) cinema:

The film, which was beautifully clear, told of adventure and robbery on an Atlantic liner. For an hour it took me away from the dirt and intrigue of Carpatho-Ukraine, and my pleasure in walking on the soft carpets of the ship, sitting in its comfortable chairs and talking to its attractive unpolitical passengers may have been vicarious, but it was none the less real. Then we came to the final kiss, the lights went up and I was back again on a hard wooden chair in a dingy cinema gallery. All illusion vanished. We pushed down the narrow stairs and walked home through the slush and snow.

Still, the reader need not fear experiencing a similar weariness, for even the political story in Mr. Winch's book is given through human beings, each of them fully alive, new to the West European reader, and unmistakably true to anyone intimately acquainted with that part of the world. Moreover the book, which is a book of travel, contains a wealth of description which makes it delightfully easy reading. Take, for instance, this description of an old Russian church:

> It was built in three sections, chancel, nave, and tower, the order ascending towards the tower at the west end, and their deep shingled roofs came down almost to the ground. The tower had two bulbous domes, shingled like the roof, and from both chancel and nave roofs spring little white boxes also supporting domes. Each dome bore a tall Orthodox cross. At the west end the projecting roof, supported by delicately carved pillars, formed a tiny veranda. While the walls had weathered silver grey the tiles were in general

rather darker, and the whole church was a study in grey shading which lent the woodwork added interest. The interior, which was practically dark, was lit by a few minute windows, scarcely a foot square, with their original roughly made glass. The building left me with the impression of something joyful, like the music of Mozart.

Or this picture of peasants in a railway carriage:

Two aged peasants, tall and aquiline, each aged about seventy-five, came and sat down next to me. They had long pipes, and pointed sheepskin hats, with the ear-flaps turned high up so that they reminded me of the Eastern raiders who had once overrun the country. At first they whispered to each other, emphasising important points by the gentle wagging of their long fingers. Then they both sat back with their hands crossed on their walking-sticks, and with that look on their faces, which only peasants can assume, of absolute detachment from the world and at the same time disdain of it and of everyone in it.

DEMOCRACY

(" *The Nineteenth Century and After* ", March 1941)

DEMOCRACY means government by the people; it implies equality of political rights irrespective of birth and wealth, and some agreed method for the choosing and changing of rulers, a power which, to be properly exercised, requires a reasonable measure of political liberty. The word " democracy " is thus made to cover three different aspects of social life and organisation: civic equality, in contradistinction to aristocracy or plutocracy; self-government, in contradistinction to autocracy or dictatorship; and freedom of thought, discussion, and political association, in contradistinction to an enforced unity and orthodoxy. But equality, self-government, and liberty are conceptions which only naive inexperience ever enabled men to postulate in a categorical form. Equality before the law and universal suffrage can be decreed, but how far is it possible to achieve political without economic and social equality? The machinery of self-government can be created, but cannot be made to work to order; and even if it works, it is in the nature of such machinery to circumscribe and, to some extent, to defeat its own purpose. Lastly, what is freedom and what is license? Where is the line between these uncertain conceptions? Although there is a deeper logical connexion between the three aspects of democracy, each of them can exist, even in a high degree, without the other two; and as each is hard to realise, they have never yet been realised together. In fact, progress with regard to one has often produced regression along the other two lines.

In England, since the disappearance of villeinage, none of the three elements of democracy was ever altogether absent. At the root of English democracy lies the right of every man to life, liberty, and property. To secure it was the first purpose of self-government: of trial by jury and taxation by consent. The individual rights of the free-born Englishman have retained their place in the political code of the nation, but in time they have come to be considered sufficiently secure not to require constant, jealous watching. Increasingly, self-government acquired an active meaning: the power of the nation to mould its common life by means of representative institutions and responsible government. But representation in an organised, articulated society cannot start on any other than an oligarchic basis: equality is more easily achieved in passive rights than in active powers.

Respect for the individual has always secured in England a certain equality before the law; respect for social superiority has prevented that equality from ever being complete. At no time was any Englishman absolutely debarred from the franchise; but Great Britain was the last among civilised countries to adopt universal suffrage. Neither the " political nation ", nor even the ruling class, was ever a close caste; but standing in the community is required to enable a man to enter Parliament, the Areopagus of the nation. Birth and wealth have for centuries been well-nigh indispensable, or almost sufficient, qualifications; and to this day they retain basic importance even under the most democratic franchise. In British politics, as in literature and art, men of intellect and abilities achieved their earliest rise under the wing of patronage, not through the support of the public; and men required in the House of Commons to think, work, and watch — purveyors of ideas, " men of business ", and drudges — were returned for pocket boroughs by the Treasury or by aristocratic leaders of political groups. Corruption of the franchise or of the electorate opened the House to wealth unaided by ancestry, and to ability unaided by either; in the nineteenth century party organisations replaced the borough patrons. But it was only the trade-union movement which, by enabling workmen to acquire pre-eminence in their own class and community, opened Parliament to the common man, undistinguished by birth, wealth, or outstanding intellect. The organised group, with its oligarchy and bureaucracy, has achieved a new measure of democratic equality in self-government. The barriers which have been raised against browbeating, jobbery, and corruption promote it in administration.

Freedom of thought in this country was always safeguarded by the national aversion against snooping — even where outward conformity was enforced, there was seldom any enquiry into beliefs; but freedom of giving expression to one's thoughts has never been altogether equal as between different social classes. Liberty, in its very nature, is an aristocratic or oligarchic attribute, possessed by single trees spreading above a lawn rather than by trees in a forest. Even with regard to political action there has always been a certain measure of discrimination. Disraeli, when comparing what was allowed before 1832 to the Whig Opposition under Lord John Russell as leader, with what was not allowed to the Chartists with Lord John at the Home Office, said that in this country even revolt to succeed " must be patrician ... although Jack Straw was hanged, a Lord John Straw may become Secretary of State ". And long may they continue to sit on the Front Bench, the Russells, Cavendishes, and Cecils, eccentric, dull, or brilliant, but always so human and so English!

English freedom and English democracy, and the limitations set on both, have their living source in feelings of respect: respect for the individual, for human rights, for human feelings, for prescriptive rights, for social superiority. This is the basis of English Monarchy and of English Christianity, of English Conservatism and English progress. On feelings of respect are built those silent compromises which render possible a civilised human existence. The Englishman does not try to enforce every right which he possesses: which is probably the deepest secret of English social existence.

The French *ancien régime* admitted neither equality, nor self-government, nor the right to freedom. The Monarchy had engrossed all power in the State. The nobles had lost their political rights, but retained their privileges — no longer an oligarchy but a caste. The *tiers état* ran the royal administration and the economic life of the country, grew rich and educated, and, except in the style of living, differed little from the nobility — yet was kept in a state of galling inferiority. The peasants worked the land and bore the heavy burdens of taxation and of feudal dues. There was the need of a great reform, but the King was incapable of accomplishing it; royal despotism had become incoherent, hesitant, and anarchical. Individual freedom was denied in principle, and tolerated in practice; and a " philosophic criticism ", inexperienced and irresponsible, developed visions of a democracy, as absolute as the royal omnipotence and as impracticable. The French Revolution attacked the last vestiges of a moribund feudal system, and the driving force behind it was the demand for civil equality and for a new agrarian settlement; to have effected these was the enduring achievement of the Revolution. Add certain political rights — freedom of conscience and freedom of speech — and here is what Sorel calls " civil liberty ", or what, adapting an expression of Abbé Sieyès, might be described as the rights " *du citoyen passif* ". Those " *du citoyen actif* " — self-government — Revolution can establish for him in principle, but cannot teach him to exercise.

" Among the ideas and sentiments which prepared the Revolution ", writes De Tocqueville, " the conception of public liberty and the taste for it were the last to appear and the first to vanish." Liberty as conceived by the men of the *tiers état* was primarily civil liberty. " Political liberty ", says Sorel, " was, in their eyes, but the instrument and safeguard of civil liberty." But in the stress of war and in the chaos " of pure reason ", the Revolution reverted to custom, routine, and precedents: " there were none for liberty, they were innumerable for despotism ". Under the Empire, the French were again spectators of their own fate, elated or harassed, but leaving political decisions to the man who was heir to the Revolution. The Bourbons had to accept the Charter. Guizot writes:

> Le pouvoir absolu ne peut appartenir, parmi nous, qu'à la révolution et à ses descendants, car eux seuls peuvent . . . rassurer les masses sur leurs intérêts en leur refusant les garanties de la liberté. Pour la maison de Bourbon et ses partisans, le pouvoir absolu est impossible; avec eux, la France a besoin d'être libre. . . .

And on another occasion he said: " The House of Bourbon compels us to be respectful and vigilant. Both these sentiments are good for us. . . ."

After the July Revolution, it was said of Louis-Philippe: " He will respect our rights, for he holds his own from us ". There was to be a throne " surrounded by Republican institutions ", " the best of Republics "; in short, a monarchy " *à bon marché* " — picked up in the bargain basement. The most passionate Monarchists, the Legitimists, were its bitterest enemies; they ridiculed and vilified Louis-Philippe, and by dividing the forces of Conservatism, helped to destroy the Monarchy. About 1850 Louis-Philippe, in exile, replied to a friend who said that he still hoped to see Louis-Philippe's grandson, the Comte de Paris, on the French throne: " You may be right, my dear sir, the Comte de Paris is possible, just as the Comte de Chambord and the Bourbons are possible: everything is possible in France; but nothing will last, because no respect is left there any longer ".

Perhaps it was bound to come to that. Royal despotism had started the work of destruction by breaking up national institutions and by reducing the nobility to political insignificance. Eighteenth-century philosophy and the Revolution completed the work of Louis XIV. Napoleon established the first modern military, plebiscitarian dictatorship. There were now those for whom French history started in 1789, and others for whom it stopped in that year. All alike talked and acted as if the nature of French society and the structure of the French Government could be unmade or remade at will. It was not easy to find a synthesis between the two conceptions of France, and few were those who tried. Nor were the chances favourable for a growth of a new habit and tradition of self-government in a bitterly divided nation. " C'est notre faiblesse et notre malheur ", wrote Guizot, " que, dans les grandes crises, les vaincus deviennent des morts." Or, even if not proscribed, they would sulk — " émigrés à l'intérieur ".

In 1868, almost eighty years after the Revolution, Prévost-Paradol sadly remarked that " the French Revolution has founded a society, but is still in search of its government ". Another seventy years have gone by, and France continues to grapple with the same problem. Of the three aspects of democracy, civil and political equality has for a hundred and fifty years been a dogma, and for almost a century a reality in French public life. Freedom of speech and writing existed to a marked degree even under certain forms of dictatorship

— this safety-valve must be left to the French: when in April 1814 Napoleon, on his return from Elba, conceded to them " a talking Chamber and freedom of the Press ", Mme. de Rémusat wrote: " Comme les Français sont mordus du besoin d'écrire et de bavarder, cela les rendra contents ". Only its own forms of self-government this most sociable and gifted of nations has not been able to find to this day.

There is a democracy of respect and a democracy of negation. The value of the individual can be put so high as to reach infinity, or so low as to touch zero: two spheres in which all values are equal.

The democracy of respect has its roots in religion, in the conceptions of the human soul and of the inner light. The nearer a religion comes to the conception of the priesthood of every man, the more democratic and levelling is its character. Modern Anglo-Saxon democracy originated in the Puritan conventicles. The more hierarchical a Church, the nearer it approaches to totalitarianism and the more compatible it is with autocracy; yet even a Church which tolerates neither freedom of conscience nor self-government by the laity, still retains certain democratic elements.

Tsarism, like some Oriental despotisms, knew no political rights in its subjects; and there was more equality, if only of a negative character, in Tsarist Russia than among nations possessed of aristocratic or oligarchic self-government. Once serfdom was abolished, class barriers in Russia were less rigid than in countries which had attained a higher degree of social articulation. Greece and Rome, the Middle Ages and the Renaissance, have left to Europe a heritage of intellectual self-appreciation and self-deception, of cultural refinement and social gradations, of which Russia remained, on the whole, bare or free. There is an inwardness and a humility in the Russian mind, a greatness and a self-disparagement, a directness and a lack of discipline, which attract and bewilder Europeans. In spite of social extremes, there always was a basic equality, of which even the curious form of address, the same for all — " A., son of N." — is an expression. The superstructure of the Tsarist State was alien and flimsy, and so are the conscious foundations of the new order; but the core of Tsarism and of Bolshevism was, and is, Russian and egalitarian, and, to some extent, the same in both.

The greatest Russian, Dostoyevsky, in a well-known passage in *The Possessed*, foretold, more than sixty years ago, the spiritual catastrophe of our time. Karmazinov, a *zapadnik* (" Westerner " — supposed to be Turgenev), explains why he has left Russia for Germany:

> Europe will last my time, I think. . . .
> If the Babylon out there really does fall, and great will be the fall thereof (about which I quite agree with you, yet I think it will last my time), there's nothing to fall here in Russia. . . . There won't be stones to fall, everything will crumble into dirt. Holy Russia has less power of resistance than anything in the world. The Russian peasantry is still held together somehow by the Russian God; but . . . the Russian God is not to be relied upon; he scarcely survived the emancipation. . . .

DEMOCRACY

> Everything has been rolling down-hill, and everyone has known for ages that they have nothing to clutch at. . . . It is only the Government that still means to resist, but it brandishes its cudgel in the dark and hits its own men. Everything here is doomed, and awaiting the end. Russia as she is has no future.

European thought completed in Russia the work of disintegrating a structure which itself was largely of European origin.

Besides the democracy of respect and the democracy of negation, there is a democracy of conceit, based on the self-adoration of man: on an enthusiastic belief in the light of human reason, the omnipotence of human thought, and the infinite perfectibility of human nature. It is the creed of a naive intellectualism, fervid and optimistic. This was the spirit of the French Revolution when its leaders set out to remake the world. Their failure produced a temporary reaction, soon followed by a new period of " enlightened rationalism ", less blatant and slightly less exuberant, but in the long run hardly less self-confident. English Liberalism and Marxist Social Democracy were its political emanations. It attacked first the privileges of birth and rank, and next, those of wealth; the one pre-eminence which it left unchallenged was that of education and intellect. The leaders of the Second International, and even the original leaders of the Third, were mainly intellectuals of a high order, appreciative of the quality which was in them.

The raving hatred and contempt which the Nazis feel for Liberal and Socialist intellectualism made certain types of Conservatives mistake them for allies. In reality Fascism expresses the egalitarianism and conceit of the half-educated. It destroys historic heritages which it hardly knows; the Nazis have swept away in Germany far more than the Weimar Republic had ever dared to touch. They profess extreme nationalism, but base it on the herd, operating with turgid concepts of " race " and " blood ", and of " instinct " as against knowledge. After every superiority has been swept away, there is nothing left but force, and as much of equality, self-government, and of human rights as force can assert or withhold. This is the meaning of Fascist " democracy ". It is the last expression of a moral and mental *dégringolade* which has eaten out the vitals of most Continental nations. Can a nation which has lost the routine of life ever find its way back to normality?

THE PARTY SYSTEM

I. THE CROWN AND THE PARTY SYSTEM

("*The Manchester Guardian*", January 24, 1941)

THE Crown can stand above parties only so long as the King does not, and need not, choose the Prime Minister; this means, so long as a clear-cut party system obviates, or precludes, his showing preferences in the appointment. The Civil Service can remain outside politics only so long as the King stands above parties; jointly they are the permanent guardians of the national interest. These two pivots of the British constitutional structure are now untouched by political strife because all its strains and swings, vibrations and changes, centre in, and are confined to, the intervening Parliamentary zone.

In the eighteenth century the King was the supreme magistrate and the head of the Executive, even as the President is now in the United States. Constitutional theory conceded to him the right to choose his Ministers, and every politician, however keen he was to force himself on the King, would solemnly affirm that he was not out to " storm the Closet " but meant to respect " the independency of the Crown ". What is more, the realities of eighteenth-century politics were such that the King, even had he wanted, could not have effectively abrogated his power to make Ministers.

Whoever presided at the Treasury held an amount of patronage sufficient in normal circumstances to maintain him in office — to preserve a majority in the House of Commons while in session, and to secure the election of a friendly majority on a dissolution.

Self-effacement on the part of the King would merely have yielded a self-perpetuating junto of Ministers, who, in fact, would have been " kings ". Therefore, whenever there was stability, the " outs " complained that an " oligarchy " of " overgrown Ministers " usurped all power and " kept the King in bondage "; but whenever there was a change, the ousted complained about an " undue exercise of the prerogative". Still, what truly Parliamentary way could there be for choosing and changing Ministers while office and patronage were the cement of politics? So far the only effective alternative to office and patronage that has emerged in Parliamentary politics is a party system, directing the votes of the electorate at the polls and binding the votes of the Members in the House.

Horace Walpole and his contemporaries saw a group of men in Parliament who, while Ministers changed, managed to achieve permanency. The politicians looked askance at them and called them " placemen ", " King's Friends ", " Treasury Jesuits ", etc. Now, too, there are men who remain in office while Ministers change: the civil servants; and a close study of the group of " King's Friends " shows that it included members who in type, and through their work, corresponded to the present permanent officials. Except in the revenue departments, there was in the eighteenth century no well-developed higher Civil Service, and a great deal of the work now done by first-division clerks was performed by junior Ministers and Under-Secretaries. Far fewer places were incompatible with seats in Parliament, and such obvious permanent officials as the Secretaries to the Treasury and the Admiralty had invariably to be Members of the House of Commons. Whatever places could be held with a seat in Parliament were practically reserved for Members, and therefore anyone engaged on administrative work who wished to rise above the low rank and poor pay of a mere clerk had to seek membership of the House.

Still, there were men whose interests, needs, and plan of life inclined them to an administrative career rather than to the game of high politics; who craved for permanency, and whose " party " was the State and not a political faction; who, therefore, looked to the supreme magistrate, the King, as their chief and were ready to serve anyone whom he placed at the Treasury. These useful men were helped to seats by the Treasury and joined in the House the significant and important " Treasury group ". They were disliked and despised by the rich, aristocratic politicians who aimed higher and who, as George III once put it, were " tho' of birth, yet not their supperiors " (true, too, they did not sup together). Theoretically it is possible to imagine a non-political Civil Service even while the King does not stand above parties, as it is possible to paint mermaids and centaurs, things which have never been seen. But in fact in this country the King and the Civil Service withdrew together from the political arena — an essentially logical development.

The Prime Minister replaces the King as head of the Executive when the King has no longer the choice of his Prime Minister, but has to appoint the man who is backed by a majority in the House of Commons welded into an organised, disciplined party. Party discipline is the key to the present system; and that discipline depends on the degree to which Members depend on the party for their seats. This is the most essential difference between the eighteenth century and the present day. In the eighteenth century parties as such had no seats to offer; Members sat on their own interest, or on that of borough patrons, or of the Treasury, or represented local groups and interests — there were vague party denominations but no real, active party organisations. To-day the number of men who can secure election to Parliament without accepting a party whip and label is negligible. On party politics in the electorate depends party discipline; on party discipline depends the position of the Prime Minister; on the position of the Prime Minister depends the detachment of the King and the Civil Service from politics. It is of paramount importance that the extent to which our present constitutional system is bound up with party organisations and party politics should be fully understood.

Every system has its drawbacks and its absurdities. A party caucus composed of mediocrities may be as efficient in keeping out the ablest and most popular statesmen as were the dullest kings; there was a Chatham and there was a Churchill, and there were blind guides who, backed by a docile following in Parliament, led the nation down into an abyss. But this must be remembered: that Mr. Churchill and the men who were called in together with him to save the situation had not, during the preceding critical years, been kept out by normal party organisations and party politics but by a Coalition flaunting the " National " label against the truest Conservatives, the true Liberals, and true Labour.

In moments of supreme danger when the nation is united — as it is at present — a real Coalition is the obvious resort; though even then it impairs the work of Parliament in some of its most essential functions. But it would be unsound, indeed destructive of our constitutional system, to continue such a Coalition longer than is absolutely necessary. In a different way this might produce results similar to those of the " single-party system " in totalitarian States: the dictatorship of a self-perpetuating clique. It is impossible rationally to explain or to defend every aspect of party politics, but if the Constitution under which we now live is preferable to any other we know of, and if the thesis is correct that it hinges on the system of organised, competing political parties, common sense bids us accept things which pure logic finds fault with. No one under our system in peace-time stands above parties except the King; in that sense he alone is " national".

II. THE TWO-PARTY SYSTEM

(" *The Manchester Guardian* ", *February* 17, 1941)

To what extent or in what sense has there ever been a two-party system in this country? For two hundred and fifty years there have been pairs of party names — Whigs and Tories, Liberals and Conservatives, Conservatives and Labour; there have been " ins " and " outs "; in short, there always were two sides. But were there two parties?

To talk of parties in 1760 is just nonsense. Nor did they exist, in the modern sense, during the next seventy years. The biggest body in the House of Commons (about 150 to 200 strong) consisted of men partly or wholly dependent on the Government for their seats or holding places — " who would support his Majesty's Government under any Minister not peculiarly unpopular "; and the next biggest, over a hundred strong, consisted of men entirely independent, who neither held nor wished for office or Government favours, the " country gentlemen ". The men " entrusted with his Majesty's business " had to look to these two bodies for " numbers ". Ability and leadership were supplied by groups of politicians, the ever-shifting and re-forming "factions": the Pelhams, Leicester House, the group of the Duke of Cumberland; the Grenvilles, Bedfords, and Rockinghams, the Shelburnes; the Pittites, Foxites, Sidmouths, Grenvilles; Carlton House, the Canningites, the Holland House connexion, the followers of Grey; ideological groups, such as the " Saints ", the Radicals, and the High Tories. There were at all times " flying squads " and intermediary formations. There were frequently problems and divisions which cut across the main alignments.

The eighty years which intervened between the first Reform Act and the Great War were the classical age of the so-called two-party system. The presence of an extraneous party, the Irish, was disturbing in the House, but not at elections. It was the separate existence of the Radicals in the early decades, and the rise of the Labour party towards the end of that period, which complicated British politics and elections and helped to preserve some two-member constituencies as a means for avoiding, on a compromise, three-cornered contests. But even the two major sides were seldom wholly unified. After 1846 there were the Peelites, and after 1885 the Liberal Unionists, to say nothing of smaller and more ephemeral groups and " caves ".

During the twenty-five years, 1915 to 1940, even the appearances of a two-party system were lacking: first, a war Coalition, followed by a split in the Liberal Party, a post-war Coalition, a three-party system 1922–1931, and then something for which it is indeed difficult to find a name, an overwhelmingly numerous block without unity of organisation or of ideas, under a leader without a genuine following — not a " lost, violent soul " but a " hollow man, a stuffed man "; lastly, 1935 – 1940, the inglorious aftermath under the " appeasers." In 1940, once more a genuine national war Coalition.

What, then, is it which has made us believe that we have a two-party system, an idea so strong and so persistent as to become very nearly a reality? What is it which differentiates the British from the (defunct) Continental Parliaments? First and foremost, the arrangement of benches in the House of Commons. The " ins " and the " outs " sit usually on opposite benches, facing each other. There is a clear line of division between them, a gulf in space, even if there is none so clear and sharp between their ideas. Location creates an atmosphere. The front benchers are the protagonists, those behind them are supporters. A challenge thrown across, an angry look, a gesture of defiance is directed against, and caught up by, the entire " side ". Even a mere removal below the gangway tends to weaken these bonds. Nor can this auspicious, apposite arrangement be considered fortuitous; it expresses the instincts — nay, the genius — of the British race, who were the first to take games seriously, and who see the game underlying even the most serious transactions; and who have made the admonition " play the game " into a most solemn moral exhortation. The arrangement of benches in the House of Commons reproduces the lay-out of a playing-field and fosters a team spirit. No one must intervene in a game from the flank and there is no place for a Centre party. The " political pendulum " swings from side to side, and has only two points of arrest.

The French arranged the benches in their Chamber amphitheatrically, and all Continental nations adopted that scheme. The Ministers sit in the centre facing both their supporters and their opponents; they are extraneous to the House, which reproduces the psychology of a theatre rather than that of a playing-field — the Ministers are like actors performing under the eyes of the Members, the public. Even Members when wishing to address the House have to mount a tribune, and thus join the actors. Moreover, juxtaposition and continuity in the seating arrangements encourage groups and parties imperceptibly to shade into each other, expressing more truly gradations in views than does the clear-cut division in our House of Commons — this is one of those clever, logical Continental " improvements " which make Parliaments " representative " and unworkable. In the amphitheatre the centre of the Government sector can be placed at any point round which it is still possible to group more than half of the semicircle: this means that there is a very wide choice. There is no " political pendulum ". At a crisis it is as if a roulette ball was jogging, hovering, on its last katabolic round: when it falls, it designates the winning number, which carries with it certain categories of minor co-winners. The same House can yield Governments in almost all the colours of the rainbow, only the ultra-violet and infra-red sectors seem to be barred as centres.

But even ideologically the semicircle expresses only a half-truth. If the seating arrangement is to express the existing continuity, benches ought to form a complete circle. The semicircle has given rise to the unfortunate conceptions of the Right and the Left, the extreme Right and the extreme Left, in appearance poles apart; whereas in a circular Chamber the Communists would sit next to the Fascists, facing across, and arrayed against, the moderate Liberals and mild Conservatives, natural neighbours. The House would no longer resemble a theatre, but a circus or a dizzy roundabout, which would appear an eminently suitable arrangement for people who cannot " play the game ".

In 1831, in the early days of the July Monarchy, Casimir Périer tried hard to make the French Parliament split clearly into a Government side and an

Opposition and to eliminate the intermediary, uncertain, shifting groups of the Centre. He failed. He did not see that if he wanted to achieve such a segregation he ought to have started by burning the Parliament building, and then have rebuilt it on the English pattern. But can any nation effectively work forms or institutions which are not of its own creation?

III. DEMOCRACY AND PARTY

("*The Spectator*", December 27, 1940)

Political democracy requires party organisations for its work. Occasionally it has had to work without them, and the results are peculiar and instructive. In April 1848, in Prussia, the elections for the German National Assembly, which was summoned to Frankfort, and for the Prussian Diet, which was to meet at Berlin, were held simultaneously and at the same places, but representations markedly different in character were returned. The voting was for individuals and not for parties — these had not yet been formed. Men with established reputations, therefore essentially men of the pre-Revolution period, were returned to the National Assembly, the more important and the more dignified of the two bodies. Moreover, membership of the Frankfort Assembly implied for these Prussians absence from home for a considerable time, for a good many at a considerable distance — it required private means. Consequently the older and richer men went to Frankfort, and the younger, poorer, and therefore more Radically-minded to Berlin; and these politically incongruous results were obtained at the same polls.

Another remarkable fact about Germany's democratically elected National Assembly was that in its social and professional composition it closely resembled the French Parliaments of the July Monarchy, returned by the very restricted suffrage of *le pays légal*. Most of its members belonged to the good middle class, were officials, lawyers, teachers, business men, journalists, etc. Of a total of 831 about 600 had had a higher education. There was not a single workman among them, and only one peasant from the Polish-speaking part of Upper Silesia. But then, in the absence of party or class organisation, social superiority is bound to prevail, whatever the franchise. The " notable " is chosen, for he alone is outstanding, whereas the " common man ", unknown outside a narrow circle and indistinguishable from thousands of his fellow-workers, cannot attract their votes unless there is some kind of organisation to direct them (hence the intense dislike which, in the early stages of political development, " notables " almost invariably evince for " party politics ").

In the Prussian Diet in 1848, among its 402 members there again was not a single workman, but 68 peasants, half of them from one province, Silesia. In the Vienna Parliament one-fourth of the members were peasants; besides, there were many Czech intellectuals and Ruthene priests who were sons of peasants, politically and socially most intimately bound up with them. But again there was not a single workman. The strongly-knit village community acted as a quasi trade-union, and where the big land-owners differed from the peasants in nationality or religion, these supplied a quasi party organisation. Similarly at Westminster, the earliest socially democratic representation came from Southern Ireland.

In February 1871, a French National Assembly was elected by manhood suffrage, more aristocratic, conservative, and royalist than any since the Restoration. There appeared " those unexpected figures of Legitimists, who seemed to have stepped out of a pre-1830 tapestry, to plunge into the water of universal suffrage and find new life and confidence from it ". " As by a miracle ", wrote the Vicomte de Meaux, " the France of olden times started from the soil." [1] But when after only five months, in July 1871, 118 vacancies had to be filled, there was a most remarkable swing to the Left and a great victory for the Republic. " *Nous étions monarchistes,*" remarked de Meaux, " *et le pays ne l'était pas.*" What then had happened? Prévost-Paradol has said, before the war of 1870, that to be elected to the French Parliament, a man had to be one of three things: an official candidate, a Red, or a big landowner. In other words, the candidate required the political support either of the Government or of the Opposition — two party organisations — or social pre-eminence. The disasters of 1870 had broken the Empire, Gambetta's failure to retrieve them had discredited the Left; when France went to the polls in February 1871, there was nothing left except social superiority. Hence the new *Chambre introuvable*, which did not, however, represent the political mind of France.

[1] See F. H. Brabant, *The Beginning of the Third Republic in France*, pp. 65 and 82.

In the next months there was a revival of political life, party organisations reconstituted themselves: the landed classes, who had long ceased to be the political representatives and leaders of the French nation, lost the advantage which the momentary eclipse of political organisations had given them in a thoroughly democratic general election.

If by some miracle or disaster a general election were held in this country without the intervention of parties and trade unions, the Parliament which would emerge from it would undoubtedly be the most aristocratic and plutocratic body ever seen in the last fifty years. In the presence of social inequalities, parliamentary democracy without parties must inevitably result in a real " pluto-democracy ".

GOVERNMENT IN WAR-TIME

(" *Manchester Guardian*", March 31, 1942)

POLITICAL systems and constitutional arrangements which were neither planned nor made but have grown up, are like living beings: dark repositories of an imperfectly known past which can never be completely obliterated. Even in new forms, occasioned by needs, dormant shapes are apt to revive — the response of the unconscious memory inherent in the organism and moulding its nature. To hunt for analogies in the past is antiquarianism; to trace continuity in its variants is history.

The question how to apportion the tasks of policy and administration has to be settled in accordance with the needs of the time and the organic nature of the Government. A sharp division between policy and administration is neither possible nor desirable — when the shadow falls " between the conception and the creation ", men and institutions grow hollow. Yet a distinction there must be. Two centuries ago the ultimate direction of policy in this country centred in the King, the supreme magistrate and true head of the Executive, who was free of administrative duties, though he could, if he so wished, participate in some of the work (an arrangement to some extent reproduced in the present position of the President of the United States). The Ministers were at that time, in name and in fact, the King's "principal servants" and were collectively described as "the Administration", not as "the Government"—for of that the King was still an essential part.

Now "His Majesty's Government" forms the apex of the governmental structure, and for at least a century past the Prime Minister has replaced the Sovereign as the actual head of the Executive. Features already present in the eighteenth century have been carried to their logical conclusion: the Prime Minister and the Cabinet intervene between the Crown and Parliament, between the Executive and the Legislature, between the nation and its Services; they share in the work of each, and are the centre of initiative in the Government. A clear delimitation of functions is not inherent either in the present position of Ministers or in its historic development.

The complexity of the system, while it at times impedes and delays action, secures elasticity — and this is one of its greatest virtues. The activities of Ministers, their nature, direction, and emphasis, can be varied in accordance with the circumstances of the time, or even with the character, inclinations, and abilities of the men. The functions of a Prime Minister who has made over the leadership of Parliament to a deputy are brought nearer to those of the President in the United States, though his position and responsibilities remain unchanged; the work of Parliamentary Ministers who no longer sit in the Cabinet, and therefore do not share in the ultimate determination of policy, approximates to that of the Civil Service, except for the right and duty of argument in Parliament.

GOVERNMENT IN WAR-TIME

Certain changes in the character and balance of Government functions produced by war mark a return to earlier forms. The co-ordination of Government with the national will, achieved through the system of representative and responsible Government, and now based on party rule, tends to revert in war-time to an older, "national", non-party basis. External affairs, culminating in national defence — or in expansion and conquests — the aspects of State action that prevailed in the past, resume their predominance; while domestic administration, which in recent times was developing in the direction of public welfare, comes to be subordinated once more to the original, external, purposes of the State.

External relations, and the means for conducting them, long remained more particularly the royal domain. Foreign policy — the Sovereign's relations with fellow-monarchs — was a "mystery of State"; the Navy and Army were the King's; and the treaty-making power, including war and peace, to this day forms part of the royal "prerogative", now exercised through His Majesty's Government. Had any of the first four Georges equalled William III in character and ability, the Ministers in charge of foreign affairs and of the fighting Services might still have truly been the King's "Secretaries". "Home policy", which in the eighteenth century meant primarily the management of Parliament — that is the co-ordination of Executive and Legislature — centred in the Treasury and, for reasons both intrinsic and historic, was linked up with finance. "Supplies" were what the Government had to obtain from Parliament, and patronage was the cement of politics.

Whoever had the conduct of the " King's business " in Parliament, had therefore to have the disposal of offices, which gradually established the primacy of the First Lord of the Treasury among Ministers. As such, George Grenville, though intensely jealous of his rights and position, did not resent first learning through the King about a talk which Lord Sandwich, as Secretary of State, had in December 1763 with the Austrian Ambassador, and which involved problems verging on war; but when the King " curtailed " the office of Court painter, Grenville "abused" the Surveyor of Works for it and — writes George III — " used this very remarkable expression, that if men presumed to speak to me on business without his leave he would not serve an hour ". " Patronage " had to be his; but as he held it from the King, he was the King's manager. Only after party organisation had replaced patronage as the cement of Parliamentary politics did the Prime Minister become the real head of the Executive in charge of the nation's entire business. With the King elevated to the non-political headship of the nation, " formed opposition " to the Government has ceased to be considered " factious " and reprehensible; and His Majesty's Government is complemented by His Majesty's Opposition.

In war-time a national leader is required to direct a united nation; without becoming a dictator, or even acquiring the independence of an American President, he holds a position unsuited to normal times (but the sham " National Government " which had existed since 1931, failed to make room for a real one in 1939). In peace-time the Cabinet is the directing council of the majority party, and consists of politicians exercising political supervision over departments, and responsible for them. A Council of State, determining national policy, is required in war, and an efficient direction of the departments; Ministers engrossed in departmental work leave the Cabinet, and men with technical qualifications — including business managers and even civil servants — are brought into essentially administrative posts. Even they must answer for their departments in Parliament, but hardly ever become party leaders. The Prime Minister, who has become the real head of the Executive *qua* leader of the majority party, ceases to be essentially a party leader, and the Cabinet, descended from the functional " Effective Cabinet " of the eighteenth century, gives up most of its departmental functions.

In the eighteenth century there was another, earlier, Cabinet based on branches of national life rather than of administration: the Archbishop of Canterbury represented in it the Church; the Lord Chancellor, and frequently also the Lord Chief Justice, the Law; the First Lord of the Admiralty, the Navy; the President of the Council, the Lord Privy Seal, and the four great Court officials added to the representation of the nobility; while the truly administrative members were the First Lord of the Treasury, for " home policy ", and the Secretaries of State, primarily concerned with foreign affairs; the Lord Lieutenant of Ireland was a quasi-forerunner of Dominion Prime Ministers in the British War Cabinet. This was a Council of State rather than a board of management, and was presided over by the Sovereign.

In the course of the eighteenth century the centre of

power shifted to the Effective Cabinet, which was based primarily on administrative departments: the First Lord of the Treasury and the Secretaries of State formed its core; the Lord Chancellor, the Lord President, and the First Lord of the Admiralty were usually in it; often one of the two Army Chiefs, but not the Secretary at War, who till near the close of the century remained a minor administrator; nor the Chancellor of the Exchequer, if he had a separate existence: before 1841 a Commoner at the head of the Treasury always combined with it the Exchequer. Between 1770 and 1812 there were only five years during which peers presided over the Treasury; between 1812 and 1841, less than one year during which Commoners filled the place; in that latter period the Exchequer acquired its high, independent position. Painstaking public finance was, perhaps, the earliest form of that domestic welfare policy, which has added, in the last seventy years, many new Ministers to peace-time Cabinets.

Which functions must be represented in a War Cabinet? The Premiership, the Leadership of the Commons, Defence, and External Affairs — Foreign Office and Dominions. (Translated into eighteenth-century terms, this would read: the First Lord of the Treasury, the Secretaries of State, and the Chief Commander, working under the active guidance of the Crown.) Finance, for the first time in British history, has now sunk from the level of policy to that of mere administration — the absence of the Chancellor of the Exchequer from the Cabinet is no real reversion to the earlier arrangement, for then the First Lord of the Treasury was in fact, and not only in name, Minister of

Finance. The Service Ministers have changed back into administrators, not primarily responsible for the conduct of the war, the Defence Minister with the Chiefs of Staff resuming the place of the eighteenth-century Commanders. (This development was foreshadowed in early plans for the Imperial Defence Committee which seated the — then two — Chiefs of Staff, and not the Service Ministers, next to the Prime Minister.)

Lastly, Parliament itself has gone back, to some extent, to the pre-party period: " factious " or " formed opposition " to the national leader is frowned upon, as it was when the Sovereign was still head of the Executive; but greater individual freedom can be claimed for a " conscientious opposition " in days when party ties are relaxed.

ENGLISH PROSE

("The Spectator", April 10, 1942)

GRAMMATICAL errors are the most primitive form of cruelty to language; they correspond to physical injuries and torture. But on the grammatical side, English is lean and tough, and offers comparatively little scope to tormentors. It is possibly the mixed origin of the nation and language which has rubbed off grammatical edges and made English less vulnerable; genders, inflections, declensions, etc., simplified to the most admirable extent, produce a natural Esperanto. But to satisfy the human need for self-mortification, English spelling offers a wholesome silent substitute for grammatical frills. Not being of " pure race ", English is comprehensive in its vocabulary. The language is like the nation: simple in forms, illogical on paper, organic but not consciously organised, and rich in resources.

Nation and language are both prosaic from choice: there are languages which in verse flow as well as English, or better, but no modern language that I know can compare with it in prose — and I possess (or suffer from) a fairly extensive, and even intimate, knowledge of languages. English prose is a perfect instrument: brief and elliptic, clear and precise, and yet offering the most ample opportunities for careful hedging. If you wish to be explicit, you can: but you can also say things without saying them, and convey your meaning safe from being pinned down to it.

Again, the language is like the English mind: clear and simple and full of suppressions, upright and yet evasive; and it achieves the most complex results in a seemingly plain, unostentatious manner. The English prose-style is an eminently social and collective achievement; its greatest landmark was the "authorised" version of the Bible, and its master-craftsmen during the next two hundred years were political writers: Milton, Hobbes, Locke, Swift, Bolingbroke, Hume, and Burke. Mr. Winston Churchill attains the highest level in speeches to the nation.

Between thought and style there is a constant and necessary interaction. Turgid thought cannot flow in crystal-clear language; a slovenly mind is not capable of a careful selection of words, so as to give to each word its full value and right connotations, and to each idea its exact and fitting expression; and to be truly discreet though vocal, free though not silent, requires skill in the use of the language. In turn, constant, diligent care of language and style is a mental discipline: it pays to undergo it. Bad writing is like bad cooking — it corrupts and wastes good material, and in the long run is apt to affect the digestion. Cruelty to food can hardly be eradicated in this country; but cruelty to English can be prevented.

Style should be governed by purpose. Where the aim is to impart factual information, a strict economy of words is, as a rule, befitting: the narrative should be terse, flow briskly, be tidy and lucid in arrangement, and yield, in its conciseness, a clear, comprehensive, and unified view of the whole. A decorative style is out of place, and as irritating as architectural frills on ordinary buildings. It may be necessary to enter into minute detail or to relate lengthy, wearisome transactions: the reader will put up with it if taken quickly across the dreary patches, but not if the author seems to relish the tedium of his tale, or aggravates it by pleasant chatter and would-be jocular grimaces. The pace of a narrative can be wonderfully altered by cutting out repetition and verbiage, even though the reduction in length is comparatively small. Some fifteen years ago, when traffic-blocks were becoming intolerable in London, I asked a bus conductor by how much a good run differed from an excruciatingly slow journey on a stretch over which I frequently travelled —and I was astonished to learn that even the worst crawl added only about one-third to the normal time. In the pace of a narrative or of a journey, as in human stature, the normal supplies a point beyond, or short of, which every unit becomes increasingly remarkable.

While the outlines of a factual account may be as bare as a geometric figure or a graph, descriptive writing, which appeals to feeling, imagination, and to the visual sense, cannot, as a rule, rely on mere delineation. We have receded from the photographic fulness and volubility of the Victorians: but the more selective the art, the greater becomes the art of selection. A fine appreciation of words is required to convey an elusive impression or to re-create a subtle atmosphere: they have to be chosen for their sound and colour, and for their even more distant connotations — for in whatever sense a word is used, it carries with it an aura in which all its meanings are blended; and this aura completes the atmosphere, or confuses it. I know a master of style who consciously varies the amount of accentuated syllables according to the pace which he means to impart to the narrative or description. But even where a slow, sluggish pace is required, this has to be achieved through words charged with purpose, and not by verbiage.

Artificially balanced symmetry in the structure of a sentence is as tiresome and obsolete as the hard-worked antithesis of eighteenth-century writers; and to leave a noun without an adjective is no longer nudism. The Greeks used certain small words to make their metres scan: but there is no occasion for ballast in English prose — accumulations of unimportant words are like fat disfiguring features. Akin to them is the stammer of embarrassed beginnings and of fumbling transitions. " Of all the far-reaching changes which the World War has precipitated in the political and social structure of European society, not the least in its importance is the wave of Agrarian Reform " — or of anything else about to be discussed. And here is a favourite conjunctive stammer: " It is hardly necessary to point out that . . ." — then why do so? Thus enriched *Genesis* would start: " Of all the extensive works of the Almighty, the first and most important were heaven and earth. In this connexion it is interesting to note that the earth was waste and void, and it may be added that darkness was . . ." There are even worse results of groping for an opening sentence than bumptious platitudes: a sudden launch and a mental bang are apt to detonate in ill-considered assertions. An undergraduate once read to me an essay on 1789, which began: " Of all European countries France alone has experienced a revolution . . ." And Sir Nevile Henderson, late Ambassador to Berlin, thus opened para. 18 of his *Final Report*, of September 1939: " People are apt, in my opinion, to exaggerate the malign influence of Herr von Ribbentrop, Dr. Goebels, Herr Himmler and the rest ". But so carefully had he examined the foundations of his " opinion " that a month or two later he wrote in his *Failure of a Mission* (p. 251): " It is impossible to exaggerate the malign influence of Ribbentrop, Goebbels, Himmler, and company ".

Handle pronouns with care. " He told him " occurs in the Bible, but should be avoided. " I think Arthur would have had more respect for George if he had quarrelled with him, as he was clever enough . . ." — comprehensible but complicated. Discussing the Palestine Conferences of 1939, I wrote: " . . . the prime movers in these transactions seem to have tried to hide their true nature from themselves ".[1] Whose nature? their own or that of their transactions? The ambiguity would deserve blame were it not intentional.

Let not pronouns outrun the nouns to which they refer: " In his speech delivered at the opening of the Home for Lost Cats, which has been erected in this important provincial centre from the generous bequest of the lately deceased Miss Smith, Mr. Brown . . ." Start: " Mr. Brown, in his speech . . . ", and relieve the tension.

" The house that Jack built " should not be taken for model. But a well-known historian writes: " The

---

[1] *In the Margin of History*, p. 85.

following account is based on . . . articles by 'an Austrian diplomat' whose name was not divulged, but who would appear . . . to be Herr Martin Fuchs . . . who was the acknowledged author of an article . . . which was published . . ."[1]

In an argument or narrative each paragraph should deal with one subject only, and no subject should be dealt with in more than one paragraph. Such discipline leads to a proper articulation of the material, and tends to cut out meanderings and repetition. Moreover, the arrangement should be such as to obviate signposts and announcements: " As was explained above", " as will be shown presently", " I propose to examine ", " I shall not discuss ", " I now pass to . . ." Indeed, even in a jumble, such notifications rarely serve a useful purpose.

English prose, however clear and simple, has also to be elliptic: at least the semblance of a free margin must be left for the thoughts of the reader. The Englishman says: " I like apples "; the meticulously precise German: " I like eating apples ". The exhaustive (and exhausting) explanations and excessive emphasis characteristic of Continental languages and thought would be resented in English as irksome, and indeed as unbearable and discourteous. The reasons are cogently stated in *Tristram Shandy*:[2]

> Writing, when properly managed . . . is but a different name for conversation. As no one, who knows what he is about in good company, would venture to talk all; — so no author, who

---

[1] See *Survey of International Affairs, 1938*, vol. i, p. 189, n. 4.
[2] Book II, chapter xi.

understands the just boundaries of decorum and good-breeding, would presume to think all: The truest respect which you can pay to the reader's understanding, is to halve this matter amicably, and leave him something to imagine, in his turn, as well as yourself.

THE END